COLOR Magic for Quilters

Absolutely the Easiest, Most Successful Method for Choosing Colors and Fabrics to Create Quilts You'll Love

Ann Seely and Joyce Stewart

Rodale Press, Inc.
Emmaus, Pennsylvania

Editor: **Karen Bolesta**
Interior and Cover Designer: **Carol Angstadt**
Project Illustrator: **Sandy Freeman**
Hazel Illustrations: **Kathi Ember**
Photographer: **Mitch Mandel**
Block Photographer (pages 26–141): **John Hamel**
Author Photographer: **Ravell Call/Saba Photos**
Photo Stylist (pages 126–131): **Jody Olcott**
Digital Imaging Specialist: **Judy Reinford**
Technical Artist: **Jen Miller**
Technical Researcher: **Darra Duffy Williamson**
Copy Editor: **Jennifer R. Hornsby**
Manufacturing Coordinator: **Patrick T. Smith**
Indexer: **Nanette Bendyna**
Editorial Assistance: **Jodi Rehl,
    Susan L. Nickol**

RODALE HOME AND GARDEN BOOKS

Vice President and Editorial Director:
  Margaret J. Lydic
Managing Editor, Quilt Books: **Suzanne Nelson**
Art Director: **Paula Jaworski**
Associate Art Director: **Mary Ellen Fanelli**
Studio Manager: **Leslie M. Keefe**
Copy Director: **Dolores Plikaitis**
Book Manufacturing Director: **Helen Clogston**
Office Manager: **Karen Earl-Braymer**

Photographs on pages 144–238 were shot on location at Ethan Allen Home Interiors in Allentown, Pennsylvania.

**Library of Congress
Cataloging-in-Publication Data**

Seely, Ann.
    Color magic for quilters : absolutely the easiest, most successful method for choosing colors and fabrics to create quilts you'll love / Ann Seely and Joyce Stewart.
        p.   cm.
    Includes bibliographical references and index.
    ISBN 0–87596–755–8 (cloth : acid-free paper)
    1. Patchwork quilts.   2. Color in textile crafts.
    I. Stewart, Joyce.   II. Title.
    TT8355.S435   1997
    746.46'041—dc21   97–4907
                                                    CIP

Distributed in the book trade by St. Martin's Press

2 4 6 8 10 9 7 5 3   hardcover

Lovingly

dedicated

to our

grandmother

Hazel

Carlisle

Atwood

Contents

Introduction 8

Around the Color Wheel 11

Color Harmonies 21

Single Color Harmony 23
One Color 24

Side-by-Side Color Harmonies 29
Three Side-by-Side Colors 30
Three Side-by-Side Colors with an Accent .34
Five Side-by-Side Colors 38
Five Side-by-Side Colors with an Accent .42

Opposite Color Harmonies 47
Opposite Colors 48
Opposite Colors with an Accent 52
Two Colors and Their Opposites 56

Three Colors and Their Opposites 60
Main Color with Three Opposite Colors 64
Splitting the Opposite 68
Four Points on a Square 72

Spaced Color Harmonies 75
Two Colors Separated by One Color 76
Two Colors Separated by Two Colors 80
Two Colors Separated by Two Colors with an Accent 84
Two Colors Separated by Three Colors 88
Two Colors Separated by Four Colors 92
Three Alternating Colors 96
Three Alternating Colors with an Accent . . .100
Every Other Color 104

Triangle Color Harmonies 107
Colors on a Triangle 108
Colors on a Triangle with an Accent 112

Multicolor Harmonies 115

Many Colors 116

Main Color with Many Colors 120

Color Workshop 125

From the Color Wheel to Fabric 126

The Importance of Lights,
Mediums, and Darks 132

Identifying Value in Fabric 133

The Difference between Solids and Prints . .134

Moving from Design to Fabric 135

Understanding Visual Texture 136

Recognizing Color Harmonies
in Multicolor Fabrics 138

Change the Mood by Changing
the Fabric 139

Block Makeovers 140

Colorful Quilts 143

Butterflies are Free 144

SpinWheels .151

When Stars Collide 158

Windmills and Daisies 166

Seascape 175

Sailboats 186

Pathways 198

Night Crystals 205

Garden Maze 212

Autumn Glow 216

Star Dance .228

Amethyst and Jade 237

Back to Basics 247

About the Authors 252

Acknowledgments 252

Recommended Reading 253

Color a Quilt 253

Index 254

Introduction

The truth is, there aren't any rules about color. There are theories, guidelines, and accepted combinations in every color book you read, but most of these can scare an enthusiastic quilter in just seconds! That's where we step in. *Color Magic for Quilters* offers easy-to-understand formulas, called *color harmonies*, for combining colors; guidelines on adding colors to make your quilt sparkle; and tips on using color to create a mood.

We've been teaching quilt classes together for more than five years, and we've been asked countless times how we choose the fabric colors for our class samples. We soon discovered that selecting colors seemed to be a stumbling block for many quilters, even experienced ones, so we decided to develop a hands-on workshop to teach quiltmakers how to make satisfying color choices by using these simple color harmonies. These harmonies work! And they work every time! Working with color should be exciting and easy, and that's what *Color Magic for Quilters* is about—it's our class lesson put between the covers of a book.

We will teach you how to make your quilts more colorful and harmonious by applying a few simple principles of color theory. Our foolproof formulas show you how to combine colors successfully and in the right proportions. These color harmonies

aking a quilt is so much fun, and choosing fabrics is the best part! Walk into your local quilt shop and you'll find quilters stacking up bolts of colorful fabric, then often asking for opinions from anyone in the vicinity. While there may be a pleasing palette assembled on top of the cutting table, many quilters need a little encouragement and advice when making the final selections. It's happened to all of us. We know what we like and we *think* we know which colors go together, but we're unsure if we're making the "right" decision. Aren't there color rules we should follow when we put colors together in our quilts?

8

are easy to understand and a snap to put to use, and they can make your quilts more lively, more intense, and more distinctive. Maybe you weren't born with a terrific color sense, or perhaps you've never taken an art class. That doesn't matter. By learning a bit about the colors on the color wheel and how each one relates to its neighbor, you can skip the technical art theory lingo and put these concepts into use for your next quilt.

Along with explanations of the color harmonies are hundreds of sample quilt blocks, mocked up with actual fabric, that illustrate the range of color choices each harmony includes. We've also added tips on using lights, mediums, and darks, a workshop on

You'll find Hazel, our handmade doll, on many pages of this book, always ready to offer a helpful quilting tip.

choosing fabrics, directions for our favorite projects, a little bit of color nostalgia, and a whole lot of magic.

We travel around the country each year to teach classes and attend quilt shows, and we always try to take plenty of fun along with us to share with other energetic quilters. We also take two special guests with us on each trip—our mom, who always adds a sparkle to our classes, and Hazel, our handmade doll, who has one ear tuned to our students, hoping to pick up a quilting tip or two. Hazel is named for our maternal grandmother, who first inspired us to quilt and often shared interesting stories about the "early" days of quiltmaking. In fact, you'll find Hazel on many pages of this book, always offering a hint, a shortcut, or expert advice to help you improve your quiltmaking.

Spend some time exploring all that *Color Magic for Quilters* offers, then turn to it each time you begin a new project. You'll be surprised at how easy it is to learn to make the most of your favorite colors, to combine them successfully, and to have fun in the process. So grab your color wheel, surround yourself with beautiful fabric, and remember that color is magic!

Ann & Joyce

9

AROUND THE COLOR WHEEL

Color, color everywhere!
Discover the magical color
wheel—how it works, why it
works, and how you can
use it to plan your quilt's
color scheme.

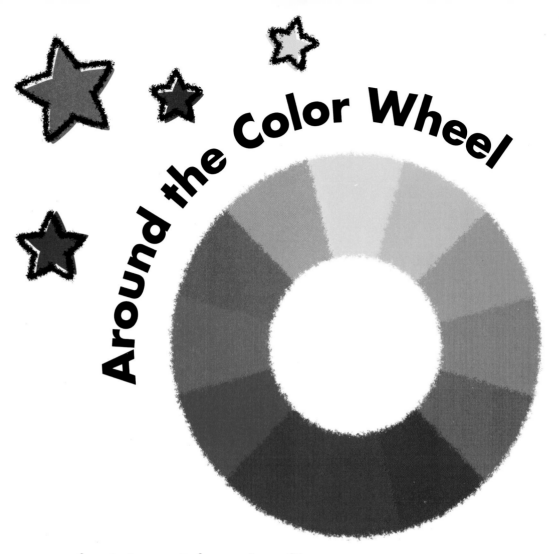

Around the Color Wheel

What Is a Color Wheel?

Color wheels have an aura of mystery surrounding them, as if they were secret tools that only experienced artists could understand. At first glance, they look complicated, even scary, and seem to hold volumes of art theory in those 12 beautiful colors. On closer study, however, you'll discover that a color wheel is simply a system for arranging color and for understanding the relationships between the colors.

Color wheels have existed since the year 200, when the astronomer Ptolomy first devised a crude color wheel. The color wheel that is most accepted today is based on 12 colors, but many artists use color wheels based on 6 basic colors, 8 colors, or 100s of colors around the circle. The most commonly recognized color wheel used for fabric dyes or pigments was created by J. C. LeBlon around 1731. His color wheel shows the colors red, yellow, and blue at equal distances around the circle and separated by three colors each, for a total of 12 colors. The colors on this color wheel are the richest, most vivid colors you can imagine and are referred to as *pure colors*.

The three main colors on LeBlon's wheel—red, yellow, and blue—are called *primary colors* and cannot be created by mixing other colors. All the colors of fabric used in quiltmaking are made by mixing dyes of these three primary colors in varying amounts. But it may surprise you to find out that not everyone agrees on the primary colors!

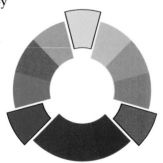

Primary Colors

The three primary colors are different depending on whether you are examining the colors in dyes and pigments or the colors in natural light.

The primary colors that occur in natural light are red, blue, and green, instead of red, blue, and yellow found in dye. In the late 1600s, the English mathematician and physicist Sir Isaac Newton discovered that sunlight passing through a prism separates into wavelengths of different colors. He arranged the colors of the wavelengths he discovered into a circle, with the primary colors identified as red, blue, and green. He demonstrated that all other colors in natural light are mixtures of these colors. Newton also found that the color of an object is a result of the light that falls upon it. By changing the color of the light, you can change the color of the object. In today's technology, it's interesting to note that the colors created for use in color television are mixtures of red, blue, and green lights. Amazing as it seems, yellow is a combination of red and green light!

Since quilting is about fabric, and fabric is printed with dye, the color wheel you will use as a quilter identifies the primary colors as red, blue, and yellow. When you mix two primary colors in equal amounts, you create *secondary colors*. Blue and red make violet, yellow and red make orange, and yellow and blue make green. The secondary colors are also equally spaced around the color wheel with three colors separating each of them.

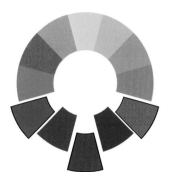

Mix blue and red for violet

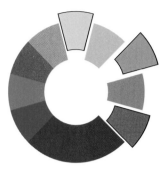

Mix yellow and red for orange

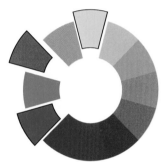

Mix yellow and blue for green

Secondary Colors

Using Tints, Tones, and Shades

how often have you used the words tint, tone, and shade when describing a color? You've probably said things like "the delicate rose petals were *tinted* dark red," "the calico dress had bright gold *tones*," or "the fabric was the prettiest pastel *shade* of blue." But did you know that the words tint, tone, and shade actually have very specific meanings when used to describe colors?

A color is called a *tint* when you add white. Tints are commonly called pastels. They have a delicate charm, almost a daintiness, and are often used when a light, airy look is desired.

A color is called a *tone* when you add gray. Tones are refined, muted, and subtle. They blend well together because they have an almost-dull, noncompeting quality to them, but it's wise to combine tones with tints and shades to keep a color scheme lively.

A color is called a *shade* when you add black. Shades are dark, rich, and dignified. The word shade is often misused as a catchall term to describe the lighter or darker version of a color, but it is a specific word that means the darker version of a pure color. While describing lightness and darkness, use the word *value*.

By mixing equal parts of a primary and a secondary color, you create the remaining colors on the wheel; these are called *tertiary colors* and fall in between the primary and secondary color used to create it. When yellow and orange are mixed equally, they create yellow-orange; orange and red create red-orange; violet and red create red-violet; violet and blue create blue-violet; green and blue create blue-green; and yellow and green create yellow-green. These 12 colors make up the standard color wheel, but when combined in varying amounts instead of in equal amounts, the number of colors you can create is endless.

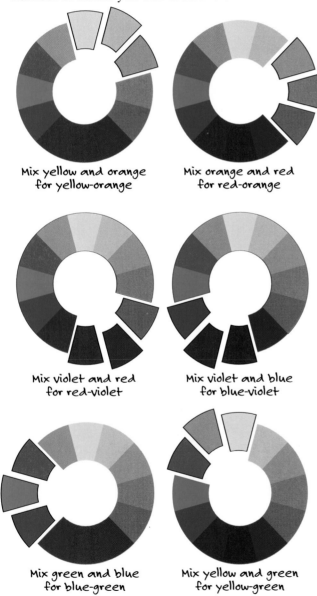

Mix yellow and orange
for yellow-orange

Mix orange and red
for red-orange

Mix violet and red
for red-violet

Mix violet and blue
for blue-violet

Mix green and blue
for blue-green

Mix yellow and green
for yellow-green

Tertiary Colors

Why Is a Color Wheel Important?

Having an organized, consistent color wheel has been a great help to artists for centuries. They mix paints and pigments using the color wheel as a guide and have made many discoveries about color interaction based on a color's location on the color wheel. Hundreds of years after the color wheel was refined, the art world still studies and analyzes the color wheel. Artists rely heavily on the standard color theories that have been developed over the centuries, and color theorists have written hundreds of books on every aspect of color use. Color theory is used on a daily basis by decorators, fashion designers, image consultants, psychologists, and anyone employed in creative or art fields, but it may be hard to imagine that it has any impact on you, the quilter.

Whether you realize it or not, quilting is as much about color as it is about block patterns, quilt settings, and quilting designs. You don't need a college degree to understand how the color wheel actually works; nor do you need years of expensive art classes to develop your own personal sense of color. In the same way a person learns to play the piano, you can learn to put colors together in a quilt. First you learn the basics in their simplest form. Then, more importantly, you must practice what you have learned. While it may be true that some exceptionally gifted people may be able to play a concert piano without ever taking a lesson and some quiltmakers seem to have an inborn color sense, the rest of us need to work constantly to achieve the color results we desire. The key to using color effectively is knowing where to begin and how to continue building upon that knowledge. Learn everything you can about color and then work with actual fabric in a variety of colors.

Color Magic for Quilters will teach you how and why colors work together and will take you step by step through the process of selecting color schemes. You'll gain confidence with each color scheme you try, and soon, combining colors in new ways will be second nature.

Color Symbolism

Everyone has a favorite color, one that makes you feel good about yourself and one that makes you comfortable and cozy. It's a color you return to when you're having trouble choosing fabrics for a new quilt project. Have you ever tried to understand what it is about that color that gives you confidence?

Colors evoke a feeling, emotion, or mood. And many colors are now universally accepted as symbols of communication—they identify charitable causes, classify physical environments, and define personality traits.

Red

Red is a powerful, head-turning color and always elicits a response. If passion were a color, it would be red. Use red when you want to stimulate, create excitement, or give the illusion of fast-paced movement in your quilt.

Orange

Orange is a very lively color, so many quilters shy away from true orange, using the more subtle peaches and rusts instead. But orange can be exciting when used in appropriate amounts and often symbolizes the human emotions of pride and ambition.

Yellow

Just by its very nature, yellow creates warmth when used in a quilt. It can be used to indicate success and intelligence or to represent illumination or brilliance.

Green

Green is the most nurturing of the color wheel colors and is often associated with the charitable traits of caring and giving. It also symbolizes fertility and growth.

Blue

Blue is, by far, the most popular color in our society. Blue is like an old friend to many people and is often used in quilts because it embodies devotion, trust, equality, and truth.

Violet

In many societies, violet is the color of royalty and spirituality. You can use violet in your quilts to convey a sense of power or to represent nostalgia, memories, or sentimental yearnings.

Colors have long been associated with behaviors and feelings and have worked their way into our idiomatic speech on an everyday basis. Oftentimes, we say we are "green with envy" or that someone has a "black heart" or a "yellow streak" of cowardice. If we feel good, we are "in the pink," or if sadness has overtaken us, we say we are "blue." We "see red" when we're angry and we look "green" if we're nauseous. We can also view the world with "rose-colored glasses" or have a "snow white innocence" about us. We live with color everyday and, as you can see, it has a tremendous impact on our daily lives.

How Do Quilters Use Color Wheels?

As you look around your sewing room, you're bound to find notions and gadgets you purchased to help make your quilting more accurate and successful. Think of a color wheel as another quilting tool. By understanding why and how the colors work together, you can use a color wheel as a formula for choosing fabric. As you delve further into the next chapter and explore the relationships on the color wheel, you will discover that certain colors can be grouped together to create an effective color palette for a quilt.

Colors can be used alone for a one-color scheme, or you can group many colors together for an equally pleasing effect. Each color on the color wheel has a relationship with the other colors on the wheel, whether they are side by side, opposite each other, or two spaces away. All 24 color harmonies discussed in this book illustrate color combinations that work beautifully together. When you study the 12 colors on the color wheel and their interactions, then use them as a basis for selecting fabric for your quilts, you're guaranteed a color scheme that's balanced and harmonious.

What Are Color Harmonies?

If you've read any books on art theory, you've probably realized that most of the volumes on color are so involved and so technical that few people could ever understand them. But if you take all of the theory and put it in its simplest form, it is about color relationships, or color *harmony,* and how one color works with another to create a perfect union.

The color harmonies you'll study are based on the color wheel. Artists have used these same color harmonies for hundreds of years. By using color relationships, or harmonies, that have been proven to work for centuries, you can be assured that the colors you put together in your quilt will give the results you desire.

Any of the color groupings on the color wheel can be enhanced by adding an accent color; this is another way of expanding any of the basic harmonies. An accent is just a small amount of an unexpected color that gives a quilt ZING! A good rule of thumb for choosing accent colors is to use one of the colors that is directly opposite (or nearly opposite) one of your selected colors on the color wheel. Another point to remember is that an accent color should be used sparingly in any harmony.

Yellow Is a Triangle and Other Theories about Color

Does color have shape? The Russian painter and colorist Wassily Kandinsky thought it did and suggested that yellow was a triangle, blue was a circle, and red was a square. He believed that a circle of yellow spread out in all directions and a circle of blue moved concentrically inward.

Does color have sound? In the nineteenth century, the French poet Arthur Rimbaud assigned a color to each vowel sound: a was black, e was white, i was red, o was blue, and u was green. Another poet of the same era identified color in terms of music: yellow symbolized soft wind instruments, orange was the brass section, and neutral white was a faint whisper in the chorus. Johann Wolfgang von Goethe, the German poet and dramatist, was even more specific in identifying color with sound. He theorized that the sound of the cello was dark blue and the sound of trumpets was red. Hungarian pianist Franz Liszt once described a composition he was writing as needing a little pink because it sounded too black; what he was trying to achieve was sky blue.

When you begin a quilt, you've probably already given a lot of thought to what colors you want to use. If you want a quilt for your blue bedroom, you've probably decided that the quilt should be blue. Of course it can be blue, but wouldn't it be exciting to throw in a few other carefully chosen colors as well? Using one of the color harmonies as a guide, you could cross the color wheel and add a bit of orange (or peach!) to make the blue more interesting. Or you could move along the color wheel to blue's neighbors—blue-violet and violet—to create a peaceful yet dramatic palette.

Look at the color wheel again. It's amazing to realize that this circular grouping of colors holds all the information you need to make showstopping, color-filled quilts. Using color harmonies doesn't mean you should ignore your color intuition or disregard your personal taste, but using them may be just the guidance you're looking for to make your quilts more visually appealing.

As you begin to explore color harmonies, you should purchase a color wheel at an art supply store. You don't need an expensive one or one that has numerous examples of tints and shades. You really only need one that has all 12 colors represented. A purchased color wheel can be a useful reference, but it can also be fun and helpful to make your own color wheel using fabrics. Working with color in fabric is different from working with color in paint or dye, so making a fabric color wheel can be an excellent self-teaching tool. You will see firsthand how fabric colors relate to one another, and you will be able to identify fabric colors more easily and more quickly. You'll also discover that solid-color fabrics have different qualitiues than print fabrics. Most of all, making a fabric color wheel will make it easier for you to remember where colors are placed on the color wheel.

How Do I Make a Fabric Color Wheel?

It sounds like a fairly simple task, but as you may discover, it can take a bit of determined shopping to find just the right colors for your fabric color wheel. The colors you choose must be pure colors, not washed out, not grayed, and not pastels. Certain colors like red-violet or blue-violet may be difficult to even find as solids. It is important to take your color wheel fabrics and your purchased color wheel with you each time you shop as you try to fill in a color or continue around the wheel to locate neighboring colors.

When we made our fabric color wheel, we purchased ⅛ yard (or a fat quarter) of each solid color we thought was right. We soon realized that each new color we added had an effect on the one next to it. For instance, when we were selecting an orange, we realized that our chosen red-orange was too similar to pure red. Each color should be halfway between the color on either side of it. Your red-orange should contain equal amounts of red and orange, making it a true red-orange. Refer often to your purchased color wheel so you don't stray too far from the accepted color wheel colors.

In the end, your fabric color wheel may not be as dynamic as you will have hoped, but the lessons you'll have learned while selecting and reselecting colors are just as important as your actual finished color wheel. You will probably see firsthand how one color can seem to change before your eyes when placed with its next-door neighbor. That blue-violet you selected may have been the perfect blue-violet in isolation, but when placed next to your violet fabric, it appears too blue. So, do you look for a new blue-violet and keep the original blue, or do you keep the perfect blue-violet and replace the blue? Either way, you may have to substitute new solids for those that don't work, or reclassify one of your chosen colors. Regardless of the individual color decisions you make, remember that the colors must work together as a whole on your color wheel and that they must stay pure and vivid to create an effective, usable tool.

Making a Fabric Color Wheel

1. Make a copy of the blank color wheel on regular-weight paper to use as a cutting guide for your color wheel fabrics. Then use a light box or other light source, such as a window, to trace the blank color wheel onto white card stock or similarly durable paper.

2. Using one wedge of the color wheel as a pattern, mark and cut one swatch of each color wheel fabric. (Since you're gluing, not stitching, there's no need to worry about adding seam allowances.)

3. Using a glue stick, glue the swatches to the card stock color wheel, starting with yellow at the top of the wheel and moving clockwise to the oranges, reds, violets, blues, and greens. Let the color wheel dry thoroughly before handling to prevent fraying.

4. Once you've completed your solid-color wheel, experiment with printed fabrics to see how the addition of a pattern can affect a fabric's color. Making a printed fabric color wheel is very beneficial because it can teach you to look *through* the distractions of the prints to see real color.

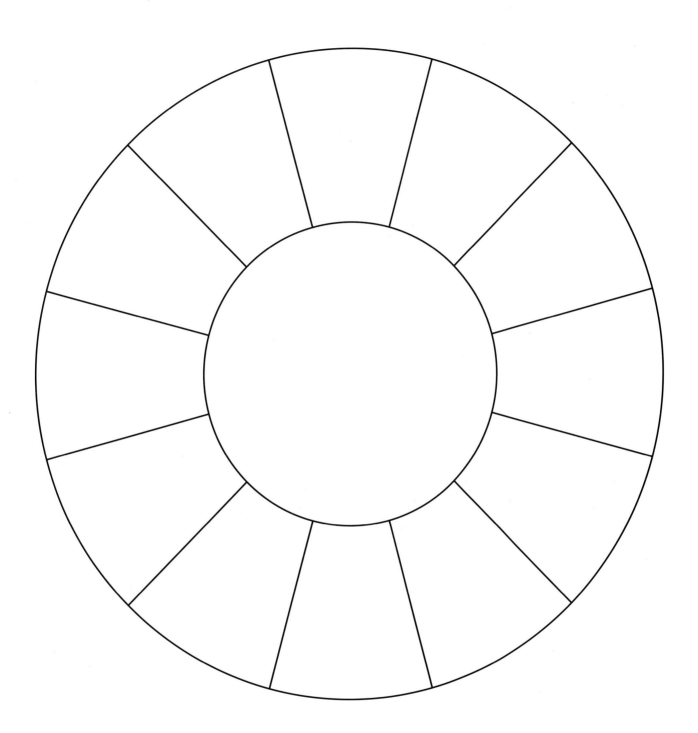

**Trace this color wheel pattern
to make your fabric color wheel**

COLOR HARMONIES

Selecting fabrics is the
best part of quiltmaking!
Keeping these easy-to-learn
color wheel relationships
in mind will make choosing
fabrics a colorful
adventure.

How to Use This Chapter

In this section, you will find detailed, useful information about color harmonies and how they work. The harmonies are presented in a logical, easy-to-follow progression, starting with a single color harmony and ending with multicolor harmonies. Each harmony is explained in simple, clear language that anyone (not just an art major) can understand. A full-page photograph of a quilt illustrates the principles of that harmony.

Once you've read about each color harmony, turn the page to discover beautiful quilt blocks showing all the possible color combinations within that harmony. These quilt blocks use over 800 actual fabrics, not computer-generated art patterns, and allow you to visualize a quilt in each of the colorways. You'll also find helpful tidbits, fascinating facts, and expert advice in each chapter that tell the story behind a block's name, explain why contrast is necessary, or offer suggestions on how to use prints effectively.

This chapter is a valuable resource for combining colors successfully. Refer to it often if you need guidance or inspiration or if you just want to admire hundreds of colorful quilt blocks. By familiarizing yourself with the basic premise behind each harmony, you'll know at a glance if the color palette for your quilt is effective, harmonious, and magical!

Single Color Harmony

Blue

One Color

The first and perhaps simplest color harmony is called One Color because it uses just one color on the color wheel. Technically, it's known as *monochromatic*; like many color terms, the name is derived from two Greek words—*mono* meaning one and *chroma* meaning pure color. But don't think of one-color quilts as dull. A quilt based on a One Color harmony can be fascinating. Each color on the color wheel is very versatile, and combining various fabrics in a single color can result in a lovely quilt.

Nature provides many examples of exciting One Color harmonies. If you look closely, each petal of a rose can be a different color red. Forest foliage is colored in endless varieties of green. These natural harmonies are anything but boring and make wonderful starting points for quilt color schemes.

The One Color harmony uses just one color on the color wheel.

Neutral fabrics don't add color, so white, cream, beige, gray, and black can be added to a One Color harmony and not change its status.

Many quilts of the early twentieth century were simple One Color harmonies, combining red or navy with muslin or white. It was a statement of social standing if a quiltmaker made an entire quilt from just one fabric.

Contrast and scale are key ingredients in successful one-color quilts. The quilt Windmills and Daisies is based on a typical One Color, or monochromatic, harmony. A mix of light, medium, bright, and dark blue fabrics in both small- and large-scale prints creates visual interest. This quilt has a "cool" feeling because the color blue is on the cool side of the color wheel. In fact, any One Color harmony will read as distinctly cool or warm, depending upon the temperature of the single color chosen.

Red

Color Options Within This Harmony

Yellow-orange

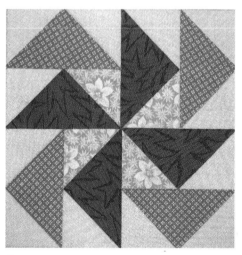

Blue-green

Neutral backgrounds are always a popular choice in quilt blocks because they allow your eye to rest between the splashes of color in the patches. White, gray, and black are considered true neutrals, and off-whites, beiges, and muslin colors are often referred to as quilter's neutrals.

Yellow

Orange

Red-violet

Green

Blue-violet

Red-orange

This block is called Dutchman's Puzzle and dates from the late 1800s. The block design was published as Pattern #26 by the Ladies Art Company of St. Louis, Missouri, one of the earliest mail-order quilt pattern catalogs. The company published over 500 quilt patterns in its heyday and continued in the mail-order quilt business until the 1970s.

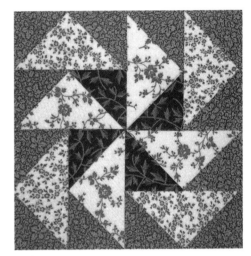

Violet

Blue

Yellow-green

Crayonbox Memories

I still remember the first thing I bought with my own money. I had spent hours in Mr. Kitchen's five-and-dime store admiring that summer's latest craze—the Hula Hoop! The one I set my sights on was the brightest shade of pink you could imagine, hot pink as we called it, and was accented with a thick red stripe that really knocked your socks off. I ran home from the store that day and quickly put together a get-rich-quick scheme.

I sold carrots to Gramma Simmy across the street (who didn't let on that Mom usually gave her the carrots for free). I pulled weeds for Mrs. Dowdle next door and she paid me a dime— probably a nickel a weed. When I had finally earned enough for the Hula Hoop, I plunked $1.29 in dimes, nickels, and pennies onto the checkout counter, grabbed my new pink hoop, and hula-ed all the way home. I think I hula-ed for one straight week.

My hoop and I were an instant hit with the neighborhood kids. I wiggled and twirled that Hula Hoop for days on end. When grown-ups tried the hoop, they just couldn't get it to hula the way I could. I tried to teach them but never understood why they couldn't make it spin like I could.

I recently discovered the faded pink Hula Hoop in the attic of Dad's garage. I took it down, dusted it off, and gave it a whirl around my waist, then watched it fall with a loud rattle onto the driveway. So I wiggled some more and hula-ed as best I could, all without success. I finally decided that over the years the hula had just gone out of the hoop because I'm sure the hula has not gone out of me!

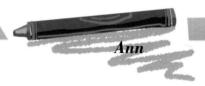

Ann

Side-by-Side Color Harmonies

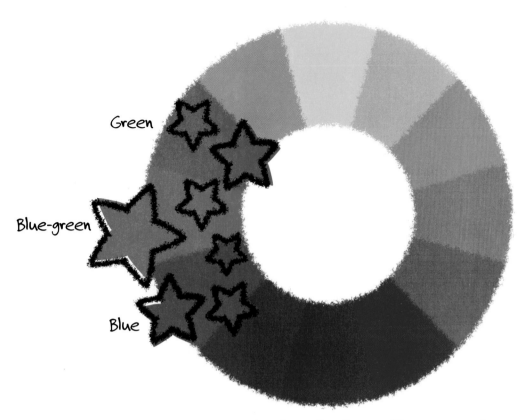

Green

Blue-green

Blue

Three Side-by-Side Colors

Colors that appear next to each other on the color wheel are naturally harmonious because each color shares a common color with its side-by-side neighbors. The colors yellow, yellow-green, and green, for example, all have the color yellow in common, since green is a mixture of yellow and blue. A color scheme of yellow, yellow-green, and green would make a pleasing quilt.

Side-by-side colors are also called *analogous* colors. The term comes from the same root as the word analogy and means similar and related, although different. Side-by-side colors are so similar that they seem to flow from one to the next, and yet are different enough to be clearly distinguishable from each other.

A Three Side-by-Side Colors harmony obviously includes three colors. The best way to select a side-by-side color scheme is to choose one main color, then add the color that appears on each side of it on the color wheel. The colors will blend gently from one to the next in the order in which they appear naturally in the rainbow. Because the colors are closely related, your eye travels easily from color to color. The result is a color scheme that is peaceful and balanced, even when warmer colors are involved. The colors are connected in a way that seems safe and natural. The deepening greens, blue-greens, and blues of the sea provide a wonderful analogous color harmony that translates effortlessly from nature to cloth. The quilt Seascape beautifully illustrates this example.

Side-by-side colors can be used in equal amounts, or the amounts of each color can be varied. Oftentimes, a side-by-side color harmony can be so subtle that you barely realize different colors are involved.

Choose one color, then add the color on each side of it.

31

Yellow-orange, yellow, yellow-green

Red, red-orange, orange

Color Options Within This Harmony

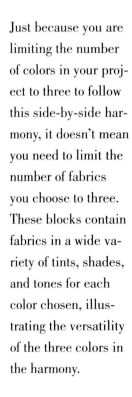

Just because you are limiting the number of colors in your project to three to follow this side-by-side harmony, it doesn't mean you need to limit the number of fabrics you choose to three. These blocks contain fabrics in a wide variety of tints, shades, and tones for each color chosen, illustrating the versatility of the three colors in the harmony.

Orange, yellow-orange, yellow

Red-violet, red, red-orange

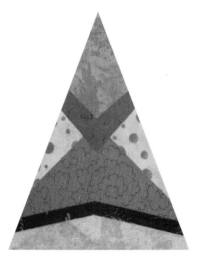

Red-orange, orange, yellow-orange

Violet, red-violet, red

Blue-violet, violet, red-violet

Green, blue-green, blue

Blue, blue-violet, violet

When shopping for fabric, you can often find side-by-side, or analogous, colors used together in a single print fabric. These side-by-side color combinations are just as beautiful in a single fabric as they are in finished quilts. You may want to use an analogous print as inspiration for a color trio, then go on to choose fabrics in those colors for your project. This method provides an ideal starting point for experimenting with Three Side-by-Side Colors.

Yellow-green, green, blue-green

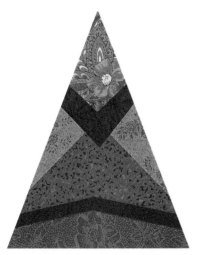

Blue-green, blue, blue-violet

Yellow, yellow-green, green

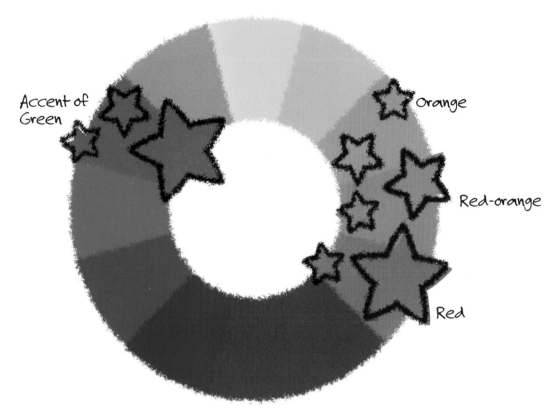

Accent of
Green

Orange

Red-orange

Red

Three Side-by-Side Colors with an Accent

a wonderful way to add sparkle to a side-by-side color scheme is to add an accent color. To do this, simply cross the color wheel, and choose the color directly opposite any of the three side-by-side colors in the basic harmony. The technical name for this new four-color harmony is *analogous with an accent*.

Some quiltmakers like to call the accent color a *zinger* or a *sparkler*. Whatever you choose to call it, a tiny dash of this additional color can turn a sometimes timid side-by-side harmony into a dramatic one. Perhaps the primary reason for this transformation is the addition of a color opposite in temperature from the basic scheme.

Most side-by-side color harmonies are focused in one color temperature. Because they are neighbors, these analogous colors tend to be on one side

To add an accent, choose the color directly opposite any of the three side-by-side colors.

of the color wheel or the other and are either cool or warm. However, once the color wheel is crossed from one side to the other when choosing an accent, a color of the opposite temperature always brings a dramatic new feeling to the color scheme.

If you study the quilt Tribute to Mother, you will notice that the three original side-by-side colors are red, red-orange, and orange. These three colors are all from the warm side of the color wheel. By crossing the color wheel to select an accent of green, the direct opposite of red, a cool color is introduced. This shift in temperature provides a refreshing oasis for the eye and adds a sparkle to the harmony. Nature abounds with examples of this dramatic color harmony. The iris, with its cool blue, blue-violet, and violet petals and warm golden highlights, immediately springs to mind.

35

Color Options Within This Harmony

Yellow-orange, yellow, yellow-green, accent of violet

Green, blue-green, blue, accent of red-orange

Regardless of the colors you choose for a block such as this, take special care when piecing, to ensure accurate seam allowances. Realistic, or representational, blocks often have more seams in one area of the block than in another, so they are easily distorted when joining the patches together.

Yellow, yellow-green, green, accent of red

Blue-green, blue, blue-violet, accent of orange

Yellow-green, green, blue-green, accent of red-violet

Blue, blue-violet, violet, accent of yellow-orange

Blue-violet, violet, red-violet, accent of yellow

Red, red-orange, orange, accent of blue-green

Violet, red-violet, red, accent of yellow-green

This block began to appear in quilting publications and periodicals in the 1930s. It is known by a variety of names, all similar and equally heart-warming—Nosegay, Bride's Bouquet, and Flowers in a Basket—and was probably a popular block for bridal quilts of the day.

Red-orange, orange, yellow-orange, accent of blue-violet

Red-violet, red, red-orange, accent of green

Orange, yellow-orange, yellow, accent of blue

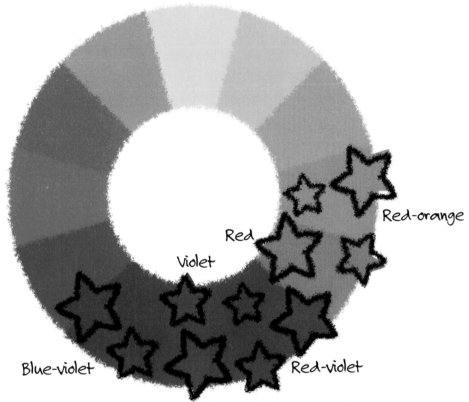

Red-orange

Red

Violet

Blue-violet

Red-violet

Five Side-by-Side Colors

Five Side-by-Side Colors is simply more of a good thing. Rather than stopping at three neighboring colors, this extended side-by-side scheme pushes even further along the color wheel to include five neighboring colors. Technically called an *extended analogous* color harmony, this scheme is successful for the same reasons as the harmony Three Side-by-Side Colors. The side-by-side colors all share a common root color with each of their next-door neighbors, and the colors flow naturally from one to the other.

In the case of this Northern Lights quilt, all of the spectacular red-oranges, reds, red-violets, violets, and blue-violets have red as a common denominator. (Remember: Orange is a blend of red and yellow, and violet is a blend of red and blue.) The aurora borealis, or northern lights, was the natural inspiration for this quilt and is one of

Move along the color wheel to choose five side-by-side colors.

many examples of this harmony that exist in the world around us. The gently blending colors of the sunset, melting from orange to violet, with all of the variants of red in between, is another perfect study. Consider autumn in New England for a moment—when the season begins to change, leaves on a single tree can range from green to yellow-green to yellow to yellow-orange to orange, and the beauty is breathtaking.

Because of the many colors involved, the five side-by-side colors in this harmony will sometimes cross the boundary from one temperature to the other, moving out of the cool range, for example, and into the warmer colors. Because the transition is so gradual and does not involve the leap across the color wheel required in the accented harmonies, the results are much more subtle and soothing.

Red, red-orange, orange, yellow-orange, yellow

Color Options Within This Harmony

Yellow-orange, yellow, yellow-green, green, blue-green

Red-orange, orange, yellow-orange, yellow, yellow-green

This harmony includes five colors, so it is important to choose a block that has enough components to use all five colors. If you find it challenging to place all the colors in a single block, remember that you can use the whole surface of the quilt to work in all the colors, as the Northern Lights quilt on page 38 illustrates.

Yellow, yellow-green, green, blue-green, blue

Blue-green, blue, blue-violet, violet, red-violet

Yellow-green, green, blue-green, blue, blue-violet

Green, blue-green, blue, blue-violet, violet

Blue-violet, violet, red-violet, red, red-orange

Orange, yellow-orange, yellow, yellow-green, green

Small-scale florals, or calicoes, have been part of quilt-making since the mid-nineteenth century. The word calico is associated with Calicut, India, and a tightly woven cotton cloth that was made there. These well-loved tiny prints are ideal for traditional quilts or quilts that are reproductions of antique examples.

Violet, red-violet, red, red-orange, orange

Blue, blue-violet, violet, red-violet, red

Red-violet, red, red-orange, orange, yellow-orange

41

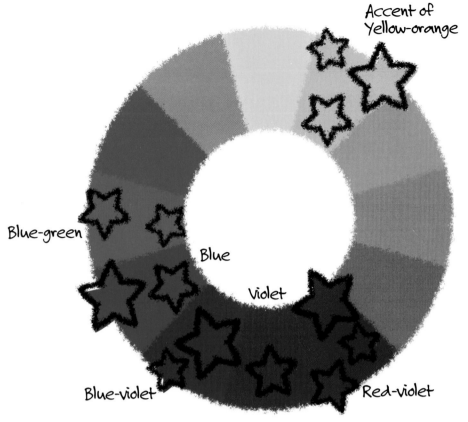

Accent of Yellow-orange

Blue-green

Blue

Violet

Blue-violet

Red-violet

S i d e - b y - S i d e   C o l o r   H a r m o n i e s

Five Side-by-Side Colors with an Accent

the final harmony in the side-by-side series is called Five Side-by-Side Colors with an Accent. While this sounds like quite a mouthful, it is nothing more than a bigger, better version of the side-by-side scheme with an accent described on page 35, and it works for exactly the same reasons. The only difference in the harmonies is that three colors have been pushed up to five colors for greater variety. Choose an accent color, or zinger, by crossing the color wheel to select the direct opposite of one of the five original colors, in much the same manner as in the previous accented side-by-side harmony.

Technically referred to as an *extended analogous with an accent* color scheme, this extended side-by-side harmony can include four, five, or even six colors. To keep things simple, we selected five colors to represent the range of colors in this harmony.

Find the middle color in the group of five, then consider using its opposite for the most pleasing accent.

While the accent could be the direct opposite of any of the side-by-side colors, the balance seems to be especially pleasing if the opposite is either the middle or the most dominant color in the original run. This is demonstrated in the quilt Amethyst and Jade. The original side-by-side colors include blue-green, blue, blue-violet, violet, and red-violet. For the accent, we selected moderate amounts of yellow-orange, which appears directly across the color wheel from blue-violet, the middle color in the five-color run. Since the yellow-orange is light in value, the resulting contrast is strong, vibrant, and visually pleasing.

43

Red, red-orange, orange, yellow-orange,
yellow, accent of blue

Color Options Within This Harmony

Green, blue-green, blue, blue-violet, violet,
accent of orange

Red-orange, orange, yellow-orange, yellow,
yellow-green, accent of blue-violet

Cut directional print fabric along the direction of the print, not along the grainline. It is distracting to see designs or lines wavering, especially in longer strips like borders. Since printing is sometimes skewed rather than straight on the grain, you may have to cut patches or strips slightly off-grain to keep the printed lines straight.

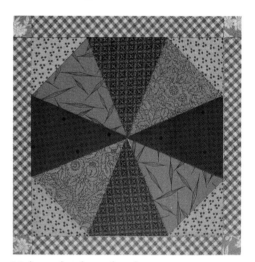

Violet, red-violet, red, red-orange, orange,
accent of green

Orange, yellow-orange, yellow, yellow-green,
green, accent of violet

Yellow, yellow-green, green, blue-green, blue,
accent of red

Yellow-orange, yellow, yellow-green, green, blue-green, accent of red-violet

Blue-violet, violet, red-violet, red, red-orange, accent of yellow-green

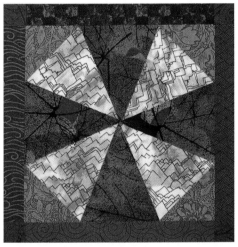

Blue-green, blue, blue-violet, violet, red-violet, accent of yellow-orange

If you find that six colors are difficult to use in a single block or think the result will be too jumbled, save one or two colors for impromptu sashing and cornerstones. The sashing will also give your eyes a rest from the explosion of color in the blocks and can work to tie the rainbow of colors together in a pleasing harmony.

Yellow-green, green, blue-green, blue, blue-violet, accent of red-orange

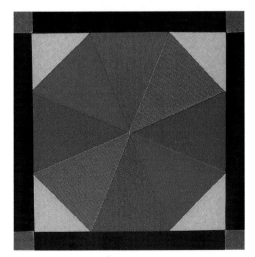

Blue, blue-violet, violet, red-violet, red, accent of yellow

Red-violet, red, red-orange, orange, yellow-orange, accent of blue-green

Crayonbox Memories

Soft pastel colors, especially daffodil yellows, remind us of our Grandma Hazel. Her flower garden was brimming with daffodils, lilacs, begonias, roses, and other varieties she tended with care. But all her hours were not spent in the garden—she also loved to quilt. She preferred to work on whole-cloth quilts rather than pieced ones, since her fingers weren't so nimble and there were few, if any, seams to quilt through.

We would purchase fine batiste by the yard from a local sleepwear manufacturer, providing Grandma Hazel with quilting fabrics in the season's most fashionable pajama colors. From the palest baby yellows and soft sea-foam greens to delicate rosebud pinks and creamy off-whites, Grandma Hazel turned everyday bolt ends into stay-warm quilts for our whole family.

She covered these utilitarian quilts with simple straight rows of quilting stitches, allowing the pretty pastel colors to take center stage. Even though Grandma Hazel wasn't a prizewinning quilter, we considered each of her quilts a treasure and enjoyed them until they were threadbare. She lived with us during her later years and spent many hours handquilting at the quilting frame in our living room. We often think of her and like to think that her love of flowers and quilting rubbed off on us.

Ann & Joyce

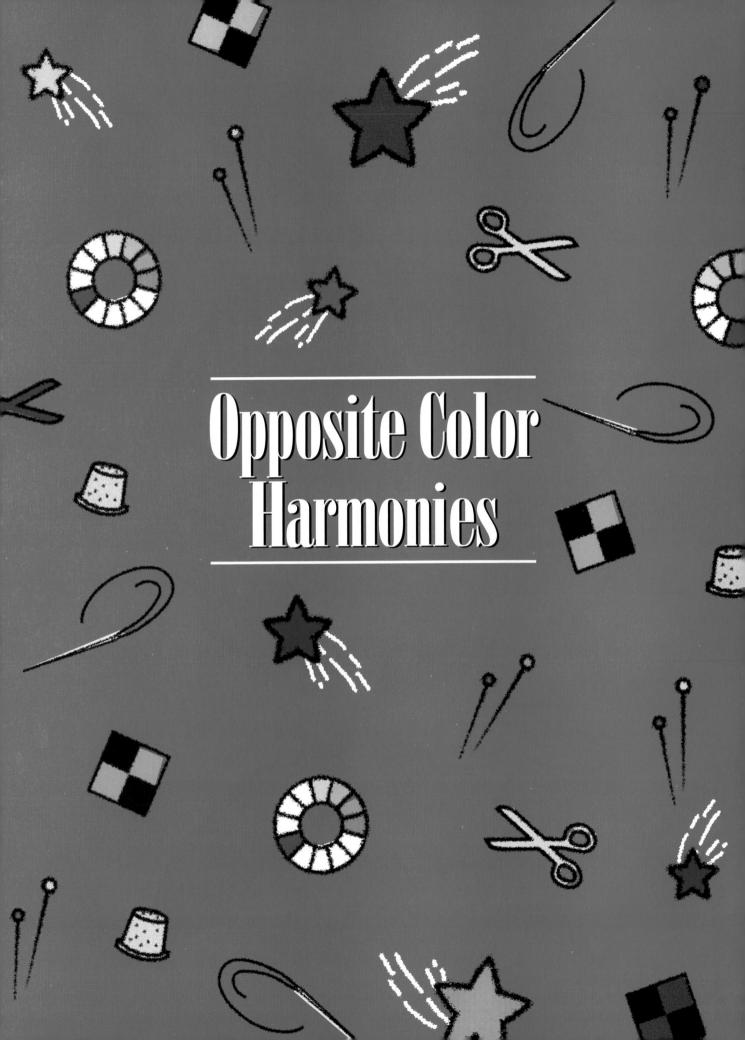

Opposite Color Harmonies

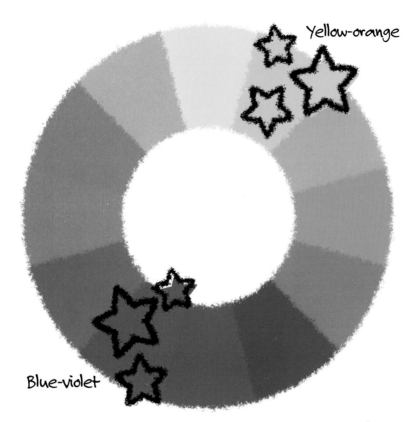

Yellow-orange

Blue-violet

Opposite Color Harmonies
Opposite Colors

Colors that appear directly across from each other on the color wheel are called *opposite colors*. As a rule, opposite colors visually finish each other because one of them contains at least one primary color—red, blue, or yellow. The remaining opposite color provides the primary color (or colors) that is missing. For example, yellow appears directly across the color wheel from violet, which is a mix of red and blue, the other two primary colors. Since each color supplies what its opposite color lacks, these completer, or *complementary*, schemes are naturally harmonious.

Because they are opposites, these colors create visual excitement and naturally intensify one another. It is important to use complements in unequal amounts. Opposite colors, by the nature of their position on the color wheel, contain one warm

> Colors that appear directly across from each other are called opposite colors.

and one cool color. Since it is so easy for the warm color to overpower its cooler partner, opposite color schemes are most visually comfortable when the cooler color is used in greater proportion. Even though green and red are easier to use and are more successful in fairly equal amounts, try using twice as much blue as orange, and three times as much violet as yellow. The quilt Mystic Garden includes the complementary pair of warm yellow-orange and cool blue-violet.

Of course, the inclusion of tints and shades and the introduction of neutrals, such as white, cream, beige, and black, can dilute and balance the strength of complements as well. The beautiful red-and-green appliqué quilts of the mid-nineteenth century, with their soothing expanse of white background, are classic examples of a pleasing opposite color harmony.

Color Options Within This Harmony

Blue, orange

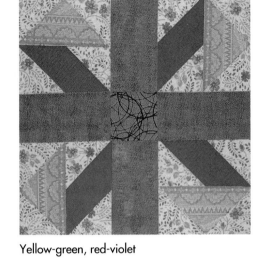

Yellow-green, red-violet

Blue-green, red-orange

Remember that all values and intensities of the two opposite colors are fair game when planning a quilt using this harmony. For example, instead of limiting your fabric choices to pure red and green, as shown here, consider choosing a soft pink and a cool mint, tints of the colors red and green, for a stunning combination.

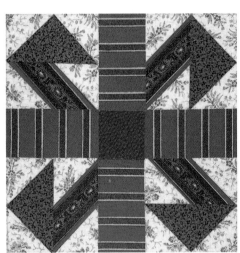

Green, red

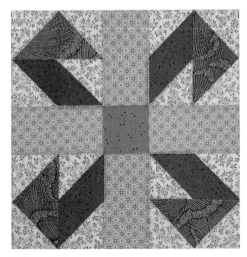

Yellow, violet

Yellow-orange, blue-violet

Crayonbox Memories

When our brother, Wayne, turned 16, he passed his driver's test and was obsessed with buying a car. So he and Dad made a deal: If he worked and saved money, Dad would match his savings. Naturally, Wayne hoped to buy a spiffy Jaguar or Triumph with the bags of gold he was going to earn. But after he saved just $200, he decided a better car wasn't worth the wait. It was off to the used-car lots as soon as possible!

While Wayne eyed the sportier used models, Dad inspected the cars that had at least a modest degree of dependability. Dad spotted the bright yellow-and-green Nash Rambler and said, "Well, son, I think you've just decided on your car and I think you've made a good decision." Wayne knew at once that he had found the car "he" had been looking for.

After returning home, Wayne immediately removed any exterior reference to Nash. He began formulating his plan to put a little spice into his first car. Most of all he wanted to change the yellow-and-green color scheme that had long outlived its hepness. The yellow was the color of chicken fat and the green was a bright lime color.

For the next few years, Wayne and his friends worked on their cars practically every day. We're sure they spent more time working on the cars than they ever did driving them. When Wayne's engine was finally up to speed, he had the car painted a handsome saddle brown metallic and had custom Naugahyde upholstery installed. He added the crowning touch in white paint—thin pinstriping that ended in artistic curves at the fenders. Wayne and his yellow-and-green Nash had finally arrived!

Ann & Joyce

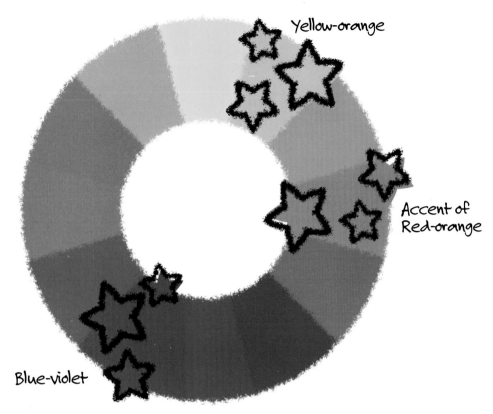

Yellow-orange

Accent of Red-orange

Blue-violet

Opposite Colors with an Accent

adding an accent fabric to an opposite color, or complementary, harmony can make an already-successful color scheme even more dramatic. This accent is not intended to be a prime player, and if used properly in small amounts, can create a burst of color brilliance. The preferred accent for a harmony of opposite colors can be found on the color wheel two colors away from one of the original colors—simply skip the very next color and choose the second color in either direction.

This accent is harmonious because it shares a primary color with the original color. For example, suppose you choose violet and yellow for your opposite color harmony. You may move two colors to the left of yellow on the color wheel, selecting green as the accent. Since green is a mix of the primary colors blue and yellow (one of the

For an accent, move two colors away in either direction on the color wheel from one of the chosen opposite colors.

original colors), it will blend nicely with your color scheme. Since there are two colors in an opposite colors harmony, you will always have four possible choices for the accent color, one on either side of the original complements.

The Butterflies Are Free quilt began with blue-violet and yellow-orange as opposite colors. We selected red-orange as the accent after moving two colors to the right of yellow-orange on the color wheel. While the original opposite colors dominate the quilt, the red-orange accent is used sparingly but effectively. The narrow red-orange border accents the butterfly print in the block centers and creates a dramatic frame around the central quilt design. The introduction of a few grayed neutrals helps this new third color blend even more smoothly into the harmony.

Color Options Within This Harmony

Blue, orange, accent of green

Yellow-green, red-violet, accent of blue-green

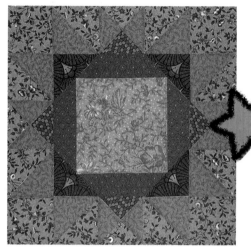

Blue-green, red-orange, accent of blue-violet

Warm colors will take center stage in many quilt blocks. Regardless of where you place them, they usually catch the viewer's eye first. Consider the warm/cool balance of the opposite colors you're using before deciding on your accent; a too-warm accent may overpower the cool color in the block and a too-cool accent may render the block lifeless.

Yellow, violet, accent of green

Green, red, accent of yellow

Yellow-orange, blue-violet, accent of red-orange

Crayonbox Memories

When I was growing up, I wanted to do everything my older sister, Joyce, did. There is a seven-year difference in our ages, so I suppose I was the tag-along kid most of the time. It was the same scenario when it came to our playthings. If she had something new, I wanted it, too.

When she was lucky enough to get a new bicycle one summer, I pretended it was mine. The frame was painted bright royal blue—a slick, glossy blue as deep as the sea. The chrome fenders glistened in the sun and the wide black tires were thick with tread.

Since I couldn't reach the pedals of such a grown-up bike, my brother, Wayne, would prop up the kick stand so I could sit on the seat and pretend I was riding all over town. I was always careful not to scratch the smooth blue paint when I climbed up on the seat for my afternoon "ride." Once on the bike, I imagined I was as independent as most teenagers. I "rode" through the center of town running errands for mom, going to the library to finish my homework, or meeting my girlfriends for ice cream cones.

Years later, the bike was officially passed to me, full of dents and dings, missing the fenders, and without the sheen of royal blue paint. I painted my hand-me-down bright turquoise and rode it with pride nonetheless, until it completely wore out.

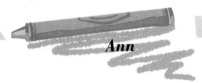

Ann

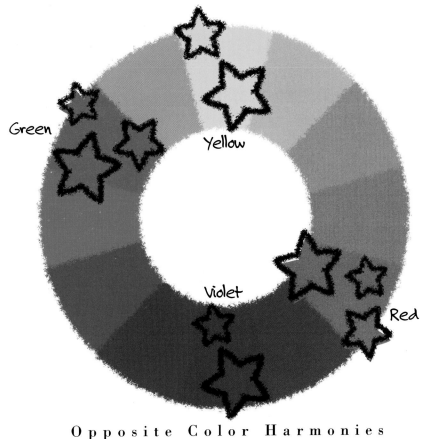

Two Colors and Their Opposites

The Two Colors and Their Opposites harmony is just what its name implies—a four-color harmony built on two pairs of opposite, or complementary, colors. These two pairs are not chosen at random, however, but are based on a familiar geometric relationship called a rectangle.

Color theory is an interesting mix of art and science. The 12 pure colors naturally form a circle—a simple geometric shape. Therefore it is not unusual that some of the most striking color harmonies are based on other geometric relationships formed within this circle.

To achieve the most eye-catching color combination for this harmony, choose two colors that are separated by a single color. Then add the two colors directly opposite, or complementary to, those two colors. You'll notice that if you were to draw a line connecting the four colors, you would form a

Choose two colors that are separated by a single color, then add the two colors directly opposite.

rectangle. The result is a color harmony balanced not only by the relationship of the complements, but also by the simple geometry of a rectangle!

Try using just one or two of your opposite colors as the focus colors, with the balance used as accents. Using the colors in unequal amounts and adding tints, shades, and an occasional neutral can result in a more visually appealing quilt.

A quilt such as Flight of Fancy demonstrates the power of the Two Colors and Their Opposites color harmony, with its complementary pairs of red and green, yellow and violet. Warm, powerful red takes center stage, giving the quilt a strong focal point. But the cooler complement of green, if used in much larger doses, will keep the red from overwhelming the design. The pale neutrals add additional balance while providing a place for the eye to rest.

Red, green, blue, orange

Red-violet, yellow-green, blue-violet, yellow-orange

Color Options Within This Harmony

Red, green, yellow, violet

For a variation on this harmony, choose two colors that are side by side instead of one color away from each other.

Then cross the color wheel to add their opposites, or complements. You'll notice that the relationship among the four colors still forms a rectangle; only this time, the rectangle is a long skinny one.

Red-violet, yellow-green, red-orange, blue-green

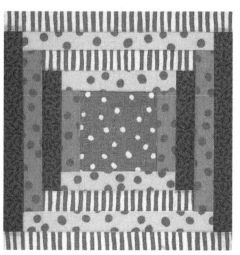

Violet, yellow, blue, orange

Blue-violet, yellow-orange, blue-green, red-orange

58

Crayonbox Memories

In the years before hair dryers and curling irons, it was common practice for teenage girls to wash their hair at night and roll it in silver-colored curlers. Despite the discomfort, we knew it would be dry and full of bounce by morning, so we performed this ritual on a nightly basis.

One summer, my family visited the Canadian resort at Banff, Alberta, and rode the chairlift to the top of the mountain to take in the sights. Because I was sure I wouldn't see anyone I knew on top of that mountain, I left the curlers in my hair for an extra few hours that day.

After the ride, we learned that souvenir photographs had been taken of each of us on the lift and were for sale. When I realized that my photograph would show those awful metal curlers glistening in the sunlight, I declined the offer. My brother, Wayne, wanted his photograph, however, so he paid and turned in his numbered ticket stub.

A few weeks later, the photograph from Banff arrived and we realized we had mixed up the tickets! The photograph wasn't of Wayne; it was of me, immortalized in sparkling silver curlers for the world to see.

Joyce

59

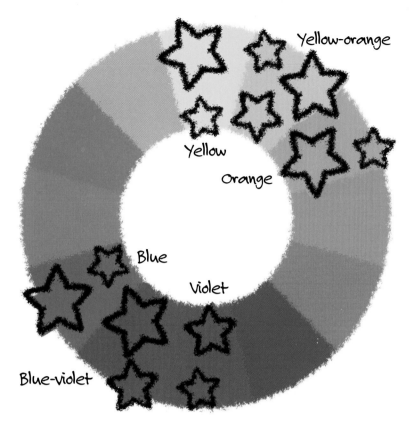

Yellow-orange

Yellow

Orange

Blue

Violet

Blue-violet

Three Colors and Their Opposites

for a rich and colorful scheme, you may wish to consider using the harmony Three Colors and Their Opposites. To identify this harmony, begin by selecting three side-by-side colors, just as you would for a basic side-by-side color scheme. Then move directly across the color wheel, and choose the opposites, or complements, for all three colors. You'll discover that the opposites form a second side-by-side harmony, so what you have, in effect, are two sets of harmonious side-by-side colors.

At first, the thought of working with six colors may seem daunting, but the relationship between these colors is strong, and the resulting harmony is extremely pleasing to the eye. The soothing visual appeal and the close ties between side-by-side color wheel neighbors have already been established, as has the strong impact a

Select three side-by-side colors, then cross the color wheel and choose the opposites for all three colors.

cross-the-color-wheel accent can bring to the basic side-by-side harmony. Imagine the results when each of the side-by-side colors is paired with its own complement, and these complements also form a side-by-side harmony. This is bound to be an exciting relationship!

The quilt When Stars Collide provides the perfect illustration of how this harmony, technically known as *triple complementary*, can be put into play with actual fabric. This dramatic quilt uses the three cool side-by-side colors of violet, blue-violet, and blue, then crosses the color wheel for the opposites of these colors, adding the warm side-by-side colors of yellow, yellow-orange, and orange. The six colors were not used in equal shares and intensities—the amounts and values of each were varied to create the desired effect of excitement and visual tension.

Yellow, yellow-green, green and violet, red-violet, red

Color Options Within This Harmony

Yellow-green, green, blue-green and red-violet, red, red-orange

Green, blue-green, blue and red, red-orange, orange

This New York Beauty block is not original to New York state. Previously known as the Rocky Mount or Crown of Thorns pattern, many late nineteenth-century examples have been documented throughout the South. In 1932, Stearns and Foster included an instruction sheet for their version, called New York Beauty, in its batting packages, and the name stuck.

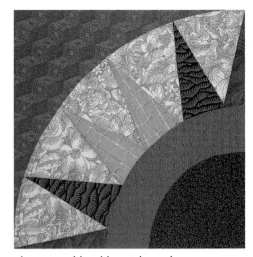

Blue-green, blue, blue-violet and red-orange, orange, yellow-orange

Blue, blue-violet, violet and orange, yellow-orange, yellow

Blue-violet, violet, red-violet and yellow-orange, yellow, yellow-green

Crayonbox Memories

I attended my first formal dance when I was just five years old. Invited as a flower girl, I was asked to drop velvety rose petals along a walkway for the dance's honorees. What fun! Not only was I allowed to stay up late with grown-ups but I also received a fancy new dress to wear for the occasion. I felt like a fairy princess in a storybook.

My pale aqua gown had a flowing organza skirt that twirled into a wonderful poof when I spun around! The dreamy blue-green color was soft and sweet and reminded me of the watercolor clouds in my favorite picture books. My dress was sashed at the waist with a narrow pink ribbon, and I wore a soft pink bow in my hair.

The other flower girls and I spent most of the evening on the large wooden porch swing set up for photographs at the dance. We sat on the swing for hours, smoothing the skirts on our frilly dresses and twirling our satin sashes around our fingers. We chatted and giggled, and tried our best to stay awake once it was past our normal bedtime, but sleepy-time yawns took over.

Many of the details of my magical evening at the dance are fuzzy now, but the color memories of my dress are as vivid today as the colors were then.

Joyce

63

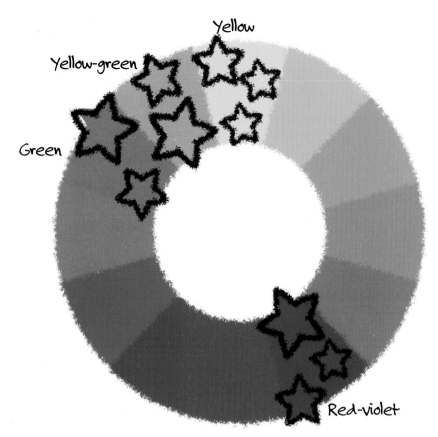

Yellow

Yellow-green

Green

Red-violet

Main Color with Three Opposite Colors

the Main Color with Three Opposite Colors harmony is another expanded version of the opposite color harmonies formula. In this scheme, a main, or focus, color is chosen, and its direct opposite, or complement, is added. Then, the color on each side of the complement is added to the scheme, making this a four-color harmony.

The quilt Romantica is an example of this color theory at work. The harmony began with red-violet as the main color, then crossed the color wheel to include yellow-green, its opposite. To complete the harmony, the colors on either side of yellow-green, yellow and green, rounded out the group. The result is an unusual but wonderfully harmonious color scheme. This harmony is ideal to use when you want colors to blend from one to another in a natural-looking floral or water design. Since the

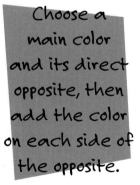

Choose a main color and its direct opposite, then add the color on each side of the opposite.

three side-by-side colors in the harmony change so subtly, they can have the appearance of a hand-dyed fabric gradation, yet their effectiveness as opposite colors is never diminished. For example, choose red as a main color and the three greens as opposites, and you have the beginnings of a red rose block with beautiful, natural-colored foliage.

The harmony made up of a main color with three opposite colors is successful because it combines the principles of both the opposite and side-by-side harmonies. In fact, if this particular scheme seems familiar, it is! It's very similar to the Three Side-by-Side Colors with an Accent harmony, particularly when the opposite of the middle color is chosen for the accent. The resulting harmony is the same—it is just the approach and the main color that differ.

Red with yellow-green, green, blue-green

Color Options Within This Harmony

Blue-violet with orange, yellow-orange, yellow

Red-violet with yellow, yellow-green, green

When using this harmony, remember that one color should play a major role, with the remaining three colors serving as understudies. To be sure your main color is dominant enough, step back about 2 yards and look at your block again. At this distance, your eye eliminates design lines and shapes, allowing you to clearly see the dominant color.

Blue with red-orange, orange, yellow-orange

Violet with yellow-orange, yellow, yellow-green

Blue-green with red, red-orange, orange

Green with red-violet, red, red-orange

Yellow-orange with blue, blue-violet, violet

Yellow-green with violet, red-violet, red

If you are planning to wash a quilt made with strong opposite colors, you may want to take extra precautions to set the fabric dyes when prewashing your fabric. To keep colors from running and ruining other fabrics, add a dye fixative solution like Synthropol or Retayne to the water.

Orange with blue-green, blue, blue-violet

Yellow with blue-violet, violet, red-violet

Red-orange with green, blue-green, blue

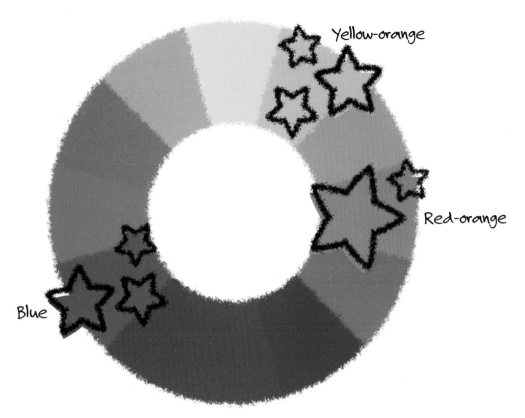

Yellow-orange

Red-orange

Blue

Splitting the Opposite

The Splitting the Opposite harmony is an intriguing variation on the basic opposite color scheme. The color combinations that result from splitting the opposite are often unusual, leading you to colors you might ordinarily avoid putting together. After a few experiments with this harmony, however, you will recognize its versatility.

The technical name for this harmony is *split complementary*. To find the three colors that comprise this scheme, choose a single color on the color wheel. Find its direct opposite, or complement, then *disregard* the complement! Instead, choose the colors that appear on either side, in effect "splitting" the complement. The intensity of a direct Opposite Colors harmony is diffused, and the result is a more subtle complementary scheme. The grouping re-

mains harmonious because the neighbors of the complement still share a color in common.

The quilt Star Dance began with the color blue. In crossing the color wheel, we bypassed the direct opposite, orange, and selected its two neighbors, yellow-orange and red-orange. Although diluted by yellow and red, orange still makes an appearance, so the opposite nature of the harmony remains intact.

Although this harmony is not as strong as a direct opposite color harmony, it still wields visual power. Designate one color as the dominant color, then use the other two colors in lesser amounts. The sample quilt reflects this approach, using cool blue in varying tints and shades as the leading color. The stronger, warmer orange-based colors are used with more restraint, resulting in a pleasing balance.

> Choose a single color on the color wheel, then add the color on either side of its opposite.

Orange, blue-green, blue-violet

Color Options Within This Harmony

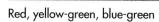

Red, yellow-green, blue-green

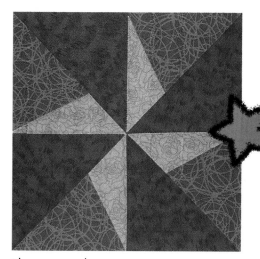

Blue-green, red, orange

Remember that all values of the three colors you're using will work in this harmony. Don't limit your choices to just pure, saturated colors, especially if you usually shy away from brights. You can successfully create a Splitting the Opposite block with pastels, darks, or grayed tones.

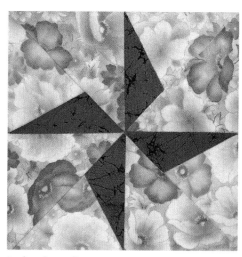

Red-violet, yellow, green

Green, red-violet, red-orange

Yellow-orange, blue, violet

Blue, red-orange, yellow-orange

Yellow, blue-violet, red-violet

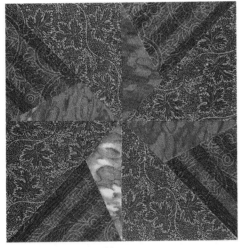

Red-orange, green, blue

Many harmonies combine cool colors (blue, green, and violet) and warm colors (red, orange, and yellow). Generally, cool colors recede into the background and warm colors advance. Decide which mood you're after, then place your fabrics accordingly within a block. Warm colors in the background will create excitement and energy, whereas cool colors will bring a sense of calm to a colorful quilt.

Violet, yellow-orange, yellow-green

Yellow-green, violet, red

Blue-violet, orange, yellow

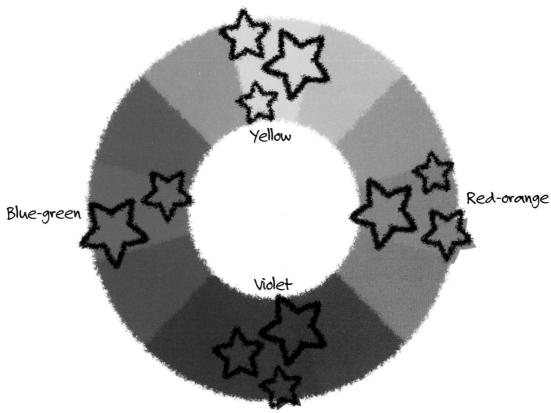

Yellow

Blue-green

Red-orange

Violet

Opposite Color Harmonies

Four Points on a Square

The quilt Hazel's Scrappy Sampler is an example of the final color harmony in the opposite color group. This quilt, with its four-color scheme of violet, yellow, blue-green, and red-orange, demonstrates the Four Points on a Square harmony. The four colors in this harmony can be determined by drawing a square within the circle of the color wheel. The colors touched by the corners of the square form a pleasing four-color harmony. This grouping is technically known as a *tetrad*.

Another way to identify the four colors in this harmony is to select a base color, then move around the color wheel, skipping two colors and choosing one, until you have returned to your starting point. You will end up with four colors, equally distant from each other on the wheel.

Whichever way you arrive at this scheme, you are guaranteed perfect harmony because you will be working with two sets of opposite, or complementary, colors. And opposite colors, by their very nature, fill in with whatever their complement lacks. In our sample, the complementary pairs are yellow and violet, and blue-green and red-orange. Since there are 12 colors on the color wheel, there are three possible color schemes for the Four Points on a Square harmony. With this harmony, all three primary colors are represented in some way, always making the color scheme seem complete to the eye.

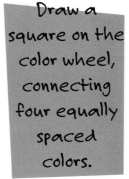

Draw a square on the color wheel, connecting four equally spaced colors.

Color Options Within This Harmony

Sampler quilts are ideal for a harmony with numerous colors. Even though these blocks use all four colors in the Four Points on a Square harmony, you could incorporate the colors over the entire quilt and in a variety of block patterns, rather than placing all of them in the same block. By varying the number and mix of colors in each block in your quilt, you'll create a more interesting quilt. You could even create one-color blocks, then combine them for a color sampler quilt.

Yellow-orange, green, blue-violet, red

Yellow, blue-green, violet, red-orange

Yellow-green, blue, red-violet, orange

Crayonbox Memories

My friend Myrlene and I spent hours playing dress-up. We had two barrels of old clothing in our basement, and we loved pretending we were princesses.

Our favorite treasure was a worn-out fur coat, as black as midnight. Its rich ebony color inspired many glamorous adventures for two little girls.

Ann

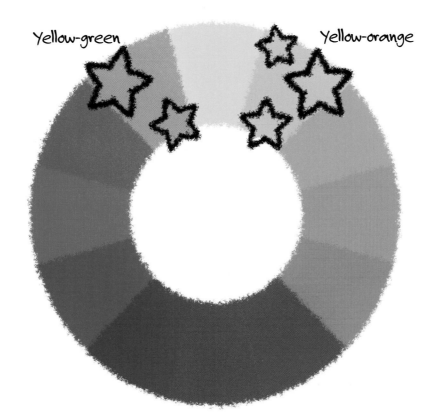

Yellow-green

Yellow-orange

Two Colors Separated by One Color

this color scheme introduces *spaced color harmonies*. This is an easy-to-remember term for a variety of combinations with technical names (and complicated explanations!) such as *inversion pairs* and *shared dominants*. To keep matters simple, each harmony is identified by the number of colors involved, and in some cases, by the number of colors in between the chosen colors.

The close relationships that exist between neighboring colors in the various side-by-side harmonies have already been examined. Relationships built on contrasts, as found in the different opposite color harmonies, have also been presented. Now, with spaced color harmonies, discover how colors work together when the relationships are not quite obvious.

Using spaced colors is similar to working with side-by-side harmonies, except that some of the

Select two colors on the color wheel that are separated by a single color.

colors are eliminated, making the distinction between the colors more pronounced. The contrasts can be strong but never quite as strong as in opposite color harmonies.

The quilt SpinWheels represents the Two Colors Separated by One Color harmony. In this case, yellow-orange and yellow-green were selected as the two colors. These colors are separated on the color wheel by a single color—yellow—which also happens to be the primary color they share in common.

Of all the spaced color harmonies, this one is the closest to the basic premise set up in the side-by-side harmonies. But because it omits the middle color in the side-by-side grouping, there is a bit more contrast than if the colors were right next to each other. There is enough of the linking color, however, in the two chosen colors to hold the harmony together nicely.

Red, orange

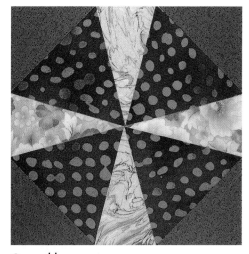

Green, blue

Color Options Within This Harmony

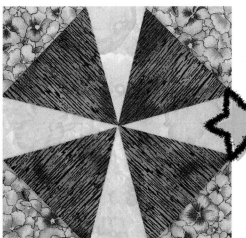

Yellow-orange, yellow-green

Blue, violet

This is an interesting harmony to use if you want to make a challenging charm quilt. Since you are using just two colors, you'll need to amass a collection of fabrics in the two chosen colors because you only use each fabric once. Be sure to include all values, tints, and shades of both colors when shopping for quilt fabric.

Red-violet, red-orange

Blue-green, blue-violet

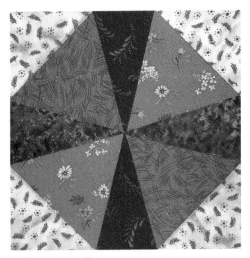

Red-orange, yellow-orange

Orange, yellow

Yellow, green

Even though you're using just two colors for this harmony, don't feel limited to two fabrics. Notice how interesting these pinwheel blocks are because of the variety of fabrics used (in the appropriate colors, of course!). Each block uses at least three different fabrics, and a few use as many as five or six fabrics.

Blue-violet, red-violet

Yellow-green, blue-green

Violet, red

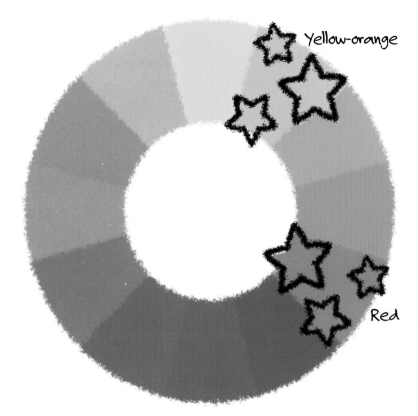

Yellow-orange

Red

Spaced Color Harmonies

Two Colors Separated by Two Colors

to determine the colors for this spaced color scheme, begin by selecting a color on the color wheel. Count two colors either to the right or the left of the original color. The *next* color becomes the second color in this two-color harmony. There are 12 possible combinations of colors based on this spacing, each ready to make its own powerful statement.

Because the colors are spaced a little further apart, the contrast between them is greater than in the Two Colors Separated by One Color harmony. At first, some of the combinations might seem a little strange, but with a good mix of tints, shades, and brights, a nice helping of neutrals, and an explorer's sense of adventure, this harmony can yield pleasing results.

Choose a color, skip the next two colors, then choose the next color.

The quilt Rosewood uses the red and yellow-orange pairing. Notice that the focus is on the tints and shades of red, rather than the pure hue.

Yellow-orange has been given a secondary role and is used in light, medium, and dark values. It might be best to use the color you are most familiar with in greater amounts when first exploring this harmony.

Since this harmony uses just two colors, it shouldn't be that difficult to find a print fabric that uses the chosen colors together. Even if you find the color combination for this harmony odd, this print fabric is an ideal starting point for selecting other fabrics for your quilt and can serve as the focus fabric for the harmony.

Violet, red-orange

Color Options Within This Harmony

Red-orange, yellow

Yellow-green, blue

To unite the two colors used within this harmony, select a unifier fabric, which contains both of the colors. These prints may be difficult to find in some of the less common color combinations, but unifier fabrics can turn an otherwise "unconnected" block into a showstopper.

Blue, red-violet

Red-violet, orange

Orange, yellow-green

Blue-green, violet

Green, blue-violet

Blue-violet, red

Avoid using too many busy prints in a single block. It's a good idea to mix in a solid or almost-solid print to break up the action. Almost-solid prints are also referred to as tone-on-tones and are useful in a multi-unit block because they often recede into the background yet offer variety for the eye upon close-up viewing.

Yellow, blue-green

Red, yellow-orange

Yellow-orange, green

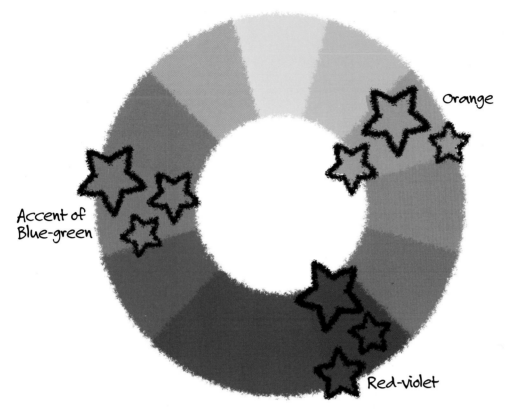

Orange

Accent of
Blue-green

Red-violet

Two Colors Separated by
Two Colors with an Accent

this color scheme definitely qualifies for the harmony with the longest name! In actuality, its explanation is short and simple. Use the color wheel to choose two colors, as described on page 81 for the Two Colors Separated by Two Colors harmony. These will be the main colors for this color harmony.

To find the accent, draw a line from each of the main colors to the center of the color wheel. From that point, draw a single line directly across the color wheel, forming a big Y in the center of the wheel. The tail of the Y will fall between two colors, either (or both!) of which can be used as a suitable accent. In a sense, you've split the difference

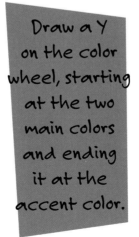

Draw a Y on the color wheel, starting at the two main colors and ending it at the accent color.

between the two chosen colors, then selected an opposite color as the accent.

Red-violet and orange were the original two colors separated by two colors for the sample quilt Charmed Memories. With the Y drawn across the color wheel, green or blue-green became potential accents for this color scheme. We chose blue-green, giving it a small but highly visible role as the lattice frame around each pieced heart block. The contrast between the warmer dominant colors of red-violet and orange and the cool blue-green accent lends an unexpected touch of drama to this simple yet effective quilt design. The multicolor fabric ties the different colors together.

85

Red-violet, orange, accent of blue-green

Color Options Within This Harmony

Blue-green, violet, accent of orange

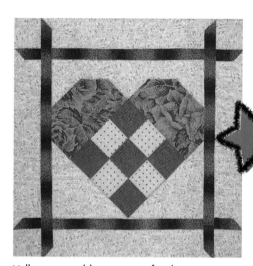

Yellow-green, blue, accent of red-orange

By mixing different styles and sizes of prints, you can add dimension, interest, and excitement to the overall look of your quilt. Bold geometric, country plaid, tone-on-tone, and tiny floral fabrics each have their own identity but can be successfully combined in a single block if the scale of the print and the color contrast are pleasing.

Blue, red-violet, accent of yellow-orange

Green, blue-violet, accent of orange

Blue-violet, red, accent of yellow

Violet, red-orange, accent of green

Red-orange, yellow, accent of blue

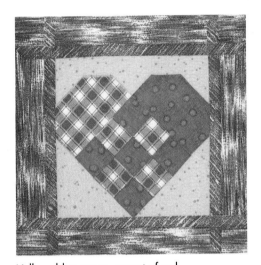

Yellow, blue-green, accent of red

If you would like to use a strong color in your block but don't want it to overpower the other colors, use it in miniature sashing or a narrow border, as shown here. Finish off the block with a second, wider border of a less powerful color.

Orange, yellow-green, accent of violet

Red, yellow-orange, accent of blue

Yellow-orange, green, accent of red-violet

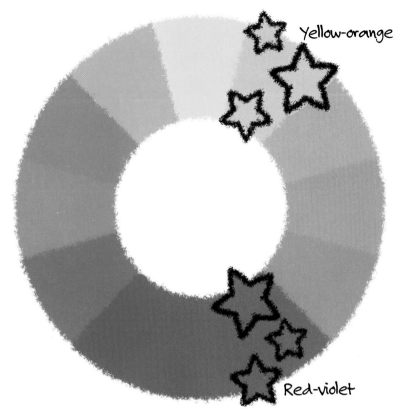

Yellow-orange

Red-violet

Two Colors Separated by Three Colors

this harmony opens an even wider gap between its two main colors. To select colors for this spaced color scheme, choose a base color on the color wheel. Count three colors either to the right or to the left of the base color. The next color becomes the second color in the harmony.

You might recognize some similarities between this and another harmony. The two colors separated by three colors harmony is the same as the Colors on a Triangle harmony, but without one of the colors! Since the Colors on a Triangle harmony forms an equilateral triangle and this harmony features just two-thirds of that triangle, another name for this harmony could be Two Parts of a Triangle.

Because the colors in this scheme are spaced so far apart, this harmony is much more likely to

Choose a color on the color wheel and skip three colors, using the next color as the second color in the harmony.

cross the color wheel "temperature line" than the other harmonies in this grouping so far. The interplay of warm and cool colors adds a whole new dimension to the design potential of this harmony and can help determine which color to use in greater amount. It's generally best to use more cooler colors than warmer colors so the quilt doesn't overwhelm the eyes.

The Star Bright quilt illustrates this harmony, with red-violet and yellow-orange as the featured colors. You'll notice that different values of red-violet are used in the quilt. The harmony seems to work to best advantage when at least one of the colors is used in two or more values. Adding neutrals into the mix will also help to keep the two powerful colors you select in check and will create more visual interest.

Red, yellow

Yellow-orange, blue-green

Color Options Within This Harmony

Red-orange, yellow-green

If you've never created a shadow with fabric before, try this block. Each point of the star contains a darker fabric that gives the block a three-dimensional look. Simply place the darkest fabric in the smallest area of each point to capture the effect.

Blue, red

Orange, green

Yellow-green, blue-violet

Green, violet

Blue-violet, red-orange

Blue-green, red-violet

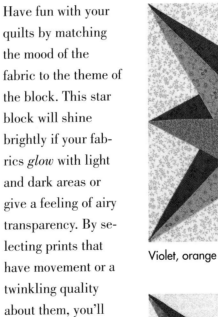

Have fun with your quilts by matching the mood of the fabric to the theme of the block. This star block will shine brightly if your fabrics *glow* with light and dark areas or give a feeling of airy transparency. By selecting prints that have movement or a twinkling quality about them, you'll not only create a quilt that's exciting to look at, but also one that brings magic to the motif itself.

Violet, orange

Yellow, blue

Red-violet, yellow-orange

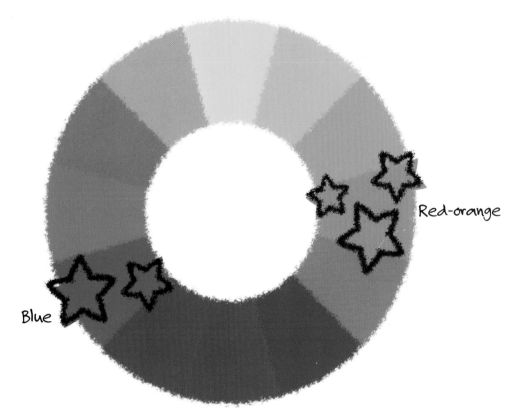

Blue

Red-orange

Two Colors Separated by Four Colors

This harmony pushes the two main colors even further apart on the color wheel. It is the widest span of any spaced color harmony. To go even a step further, separating by five colors, would move the combination into the opposite color category.

To select colors for the Two Colors Separated by Four Colors harmony, begin by choosing a color on the color wheel. Count four colors either to the left or to the right of the original color, then use the *next* color for this two-color harmony.

When you use Two Colors Separated by Four Colors as the basis for your color scheme, one of the colors always includes a little bit of its opposite, or complementary, color. This makes for a very pleasing combination. For example, if you choose

Choose a color on the color wheel, skip four colors, and use the next color.

red as your starting color, the two options for this harmony would be yellow-green or blue-green. Either choice contains green, the direct complement of red, but without the full-strength impact of the direct opposite pairing. In fact, you might call this color harmony just a little off-center!

As with the Two Colors Separated by Three Colors harmony, the span between the two colors is wide enough to cross the color wheel's cool/warm line. When this crossover occurs, the resulting temperature contrast adds extra excitement to an already intriguing pairing.

The quilt Welcome includes the colors cool blue and a light value of warm red-orange. To maintain a sense of balance, we used the cooler color in greater proportion to the warmer hue.

Red, yellow-green

Yellow-orange, blue

Color Options Within This Harmony

Violet, yellow-orange

By varying the placement of color within this Pineapple block, you can design an unlimited number of settings, especially when you repeat colors in the outer "logs" to resemble a border. A variation of the basic Log Cabin block, this Pineapple version creates a stunning pattern of overlapping color, giving the illusion of over-and-under tucking of fabric.

Yellow, blue-violet

Orange, blue-green

Blue-green, red

94

Green, red-violet

Blue-violet, orange

Yellow-green, violet

Even though this harmony uses only two colors, try using three or four fabrics of each color in a block. For example, freely mix light yellow-greens with medium and dark yellow-greens, and add yellow-greens with neutral backgrounds to give a scrappy feel to a planned color scheme.

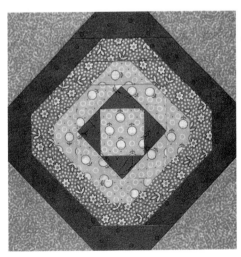

Red-orange, green

Blue, red-orange

Red-violet, yellow

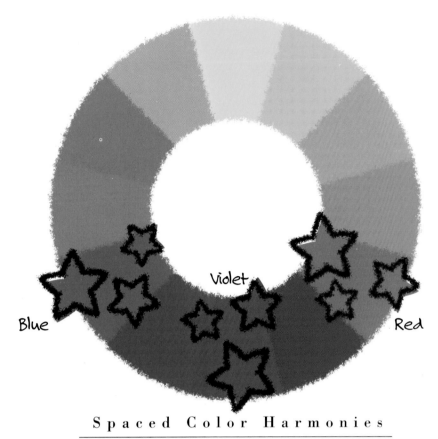

Blue

Violet

Red

Three Alternating Colors

t his harmony is similar to a Five Side-by-Side Colors harmony, except that every other color is eliminated. This gives it the closeness of the side-by-side scheme, but with a little less subtlety and a little more pep, because the actual "linking" colors have been omitted.

To identify this harmony, select a single color on the color wheel. Moving in either direction, bypass the neighboring color, but choose the next color. Repeat, using this second color as the starting point. You are, in essence, picking one, then skipping one, until you have chosen three colors. In many cases, the harmony will contain both cool and warm colors, which will add to the visual excitement of the three chosen colors.

An example of this harmony is yellow (skip yellow-green), green (skip blue-green), and blue.

Pick one color, skip one color, and repeat until you have three colors.

Although the linking colors are missing, the remaining colors are still connected because green, the middle color, is a mix of the other two.

Another example can be found in the color scheme for the quilt Five Baskets. This *colorway*, or color combination, includes red (skip red-violet), violet (skip blue-violet), and blue. Violet, the middle color, results from mixing the two end colors in the harmony, red and blue. The scheme includes cool blue and violet, as well as warm red in a variety of tints, tones, and shades.

It would be best to choose one color as the main color when working in this harmony, especially if you are using a block with a great deal of background. The remaining two colors of fabrics should be strong in value contrast so the main color doesn't overwhelm.

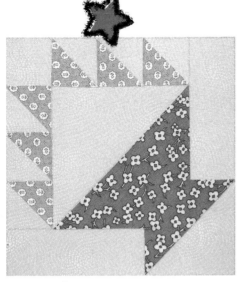

Orange, yellow, green

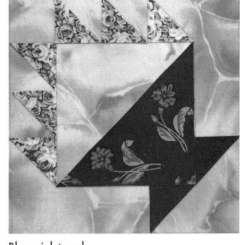

Blue, violet, red

Color Options Within This Harmony

Yellow, green, blue

If the color combinations in this harmony seem overpowering, consider using a neutral fabric as a background in the block to tone down the colors. Choose white to soften colors or make them appear more delicate, gray to reduce the vibrance of a color, and off-whites and light tans to give the eye a resting spot.

Violet, red, orange

Green, blue, violet

Red, orange, yellow

Red-orange, yellow-orange, yellow-green

Blue-green, blue-violet, red-violet

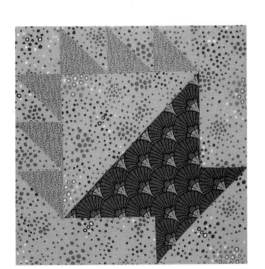

Yellow-orange, yellow-green, blue-green

Basket quilts can be traced back to the mid-1800s. Broderie Perse was all the rage, so ladies of the era cut basket and flower shapes from beautiful chintzes, appliquéd them onto quilt tops, then accented them with embroidery. Pieced baskets emerged as one of the most popular block designs of the 1920s, when quiltmaking enjoyed a resurgence in America.

Blue-violet, red-violet, red-orange

Yellow-green, blue-green, blue-violet

Red-violet, red-orange, yellow-orange

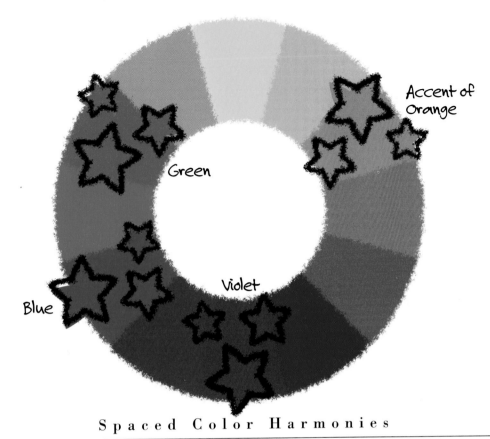

Green

Accent of Orange

Violet

Blue

Three Alternating Colors with an Accent

t o add an extra touch of spice to this spaced color harmony, cross the color wheel and select the direct opposite of the middle color in the three-color group to fill out the Three Alternating Colors with an Accent harmony. The addition of this contrasting accent brings visual tension and excitement to the basic three alternating colors harmony.

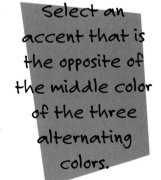

Select an accent that is the opposite of the middle color of the three alternating colors.

The three alternating colors of green, blue, and violet were selected by identifying a single color on the color wheel—in this case, green. We moved two colors away, bypassing the neighboring color blue-green, and chose blue. We then bypassed blue-violet and chose violet. Adding the accent brought a whole new dimension to the previously explored Three Alternating Colors harmony.

Sometimes called a sparkler or a zinger, the accent color in this harmony keeps the eye moving and adds a little pep to boot. Yet, the accent is so natural, it seems to belong as much as each of the three alternating colors originally selected.

You can see what the addition of orange does for the overall impact of the Sailboats quilt. The orange sails not only inject life, but also bring a touch of warmth to the otherwise cool color scheme of green, blue, and violet. We selected orange as the accent color because it is the direct opposite of blue, the middle color in our original trio. We've used it sparingly, as befits any accent color. Here, it suggests the light reflecting off the boat's sails, creating a playful, sunny effect.

Color Options Within This Harmony

Orange, yellow, green, accent of violet

Blue, violet, red, accent of yellow

Yellow, green, blue, accent of red

Keep your eyes open for conversational or realistic prints when planning a sailboat quilt. Woodgrain prints are perfect for re-creating a classic-style boat, and watercolor sky, swirling cloud designs, and wave prints could be used for the background. By carefully selecting colors and prints, you could create different moods for this seaside scene—dark and stormy, clear and breezy, or kid-bright and full of fun.

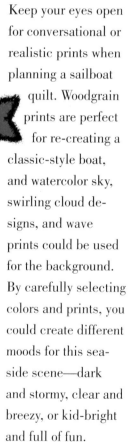

Violet, red, orange, accent of green

Green, blue, violet, accent of orange

Red, orange, yellow, accent of blue

Yellow-orange, yellow-green, blue-green, accent of red-violet

Blue-violet, red-violet, red-orange, accent of yellow-green

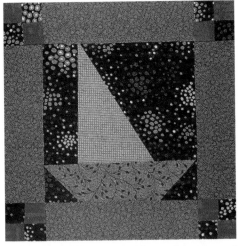

Yellow-green, blue-green, blue-violet, accent of red-orange

When exploring different colorways for this harmony, you may want to make sample blocks before committing to a scheme for your whole quilt. Experimenting with colors and fabrics is especially important if you're working with a color you don't normally use, such as orange or yellow-green, since your fabric stash may contain few, if any, fabrics in these colors.

Red-violet, red-orange, yellow-orange, accent of blue-green

Blue-green, blue-violet, red-violet, accent of yellow-orange

Red-orange, yellow-orange, yellow-green, accent of blue-violet

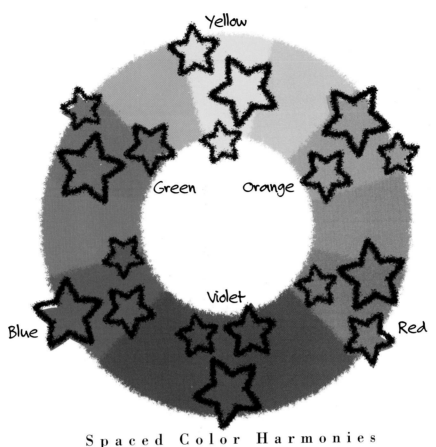

Yellow

Green

Orange

Blue

Violet

Red

S p a c e d C o l o r H a r m o n i e s

Every Other Color

Last but certainly not least in the family of spaced color harmonies is the Every Other Color harmony. It is technically known as *full range of alternates* harmony because it includes alternating colors around the color wheel. If you circle the color wheel, choosing every other color, you will have identified the six colors in this vibrant harmony.

There are two possible color schemes for this harmony. One includes all the primary and secondary colors—red, yellow, blue, orange, green, and violet. The other scheme has all the mixed colors—red-orange, yellow-orange, yellow-green, blue-green, blue-violet, and red-violet. It is easy to see the relationships between the colors in each of these two groupings, so we can understand why they are harmonious. In each

case, the grouping includes a wonderful balance of warm and cool colors, all equally distant from one another on the color wheel.

Quilts that result from the use of this harmony are bound to be exciting and colorful. If you showcase the tints of the colors, the results are subtle and delicate. By focusing on the darker shades, you can create a sense of mystery or contemplation. Or, if you select the pure color wheel hues, as shown in the Night Crystals quilt, the results can be bold and flashy. Choosing a dark, star-studded neutral for a background heightens this colorful effect. Using white or cream with the colors in this harmony would also provide a diffusing effect, lessening the jolt of color-splashed fabrics in a block or quilt.

Move around the color wheel, choosing every other color.

105

Color Options Within This Harmony

Red, orange, yellow, green, blue, violet

Red-orange, yellow-orange, yellow-green, blue-green, blue-violet, red-violet

You can easily achieve two distinct looks for this block just by changing value placement. Play up the center area of the block by using strong pure colors, then select a neutral for the background. Or focus on the block as a whole by keeping the values consistent throughout the patchwork pieces.

Crayonbox Memories

When I was two, Mom knitted a darling ensemble for me. The lacy dress and brimmed hat were made of a soft baby yarn in the palest of pinks, since pink has always been a favorite color for little girls. Mom loves to knit and has been president of her knitting club for almost 50 years!

Joyce

Triangle Color Harmonies

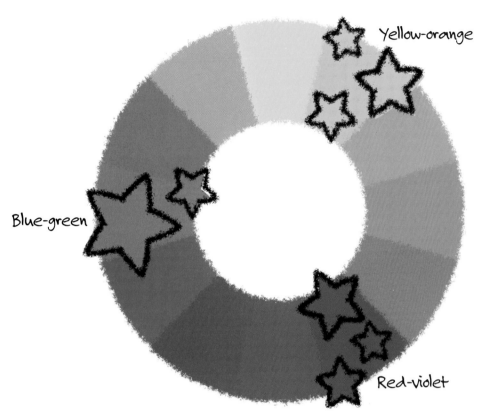

Yellow-orange

Blue-green

Red-violet

Colors on a Triangle

Color harmonies using rectangles and squares rotated around the color wheel have already been presented. The final scheme based on a familiar geometric arrangement is called the Colors on a Triangle harmony. Technically known as a *triad*, the three colors that form this harmonious trio are easy to identify. Choose any three colors equally distant from each other on the color wheel. These colors do not share the properties of direct opposites, nor are they related by common colors in the manner of side-by-side harmonies. Yet they are beautifully balanced and very "economical," giving the illusion of full color with just three ingredients!

There are two ways to determine the various schemes for this harmony. One is to draw an equilateral triangle (all sides are equal) inside the color wheel. The three colors touched by the points of

Use three colors equally distant from each other on the color wheel.

this triangle will be equally spaced around the wheel. The other way is to select a base color, then proceed around the color wheel, skipping three colors and choosing one, until you are back at your starting point.

Because there are 12 colors on the color wheel, there are four possible colorways. The first is made up of the three primary colors of red, yellow, and blue. The second is comprised of the three secondary colors of orange, green, and violet. Each of the final two is formed using three tertiary colors.

The quilt Mardi Gras uses the tertiary combination of yellow-orange, blue-green, and red-violet to create its vibrant and colorful image. Cool, serene blue-green is the dominant color and creates an ethereal mood, while the two warmer hues of yellow-orange and red-violet are used more sparingly and add a splash of color.

Color Options Within This Harmony

Orange, green, violet

Yellow, blue, red

Yellow-orange, blue-green, red-violet

Yellow-green, blue-violet, red-orange

Scrap-style quilts, combining dozens of different fabrics, have almost become the norm. Yet many quilters still rely on the proven success of a uniform color scheme that uses just three or four fabrics.

Try large-scale prints in small areas. The full motif may be lost in the cutting, but you'll gain new interest on the printed design that is even better than what was intended by the fabric designer.

Crayonbox Memories

Each summer, Dad planted a huge vegetable garden, and I would watch in awe as the light green shoots popped through the earth, then turned into lush greenery almost overnight. When I was about seven, I was bursting with enthusiasm for growing and begged Dad to let me plant something for myself. Careful not to discourage a budding gardener, Dad gave me a handful of castor bean seeds and sectioned off a small plot of ground under my bedroom window.

I pushed the seeds into the soft, moist ground with my little fingers, then I covered them with layers of dirt. I didn't have to wait long for my seeds to sprout. I dumped gallon after gallon of water on my seedlings, yet they continued their growing spurt. I tended my garden with care and soon my castor bean plants had grown taller than I. The leaves were a rich dark green and so large and full that I could easily disappear behind them during games of Hide and Seek.

I was so proud of myself since I thought that I had singlehandedly made my plants grow so healthy and huge. I showed off my beautiful green garden to everyone and considered myself a master gardener. As the summer wore on, the vibrant greens in my castor bean plants started to fade to yellow, but my determination to grow an even bigger castor bean plant the next year continued to flourish.

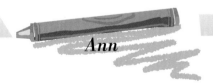

Ann

111

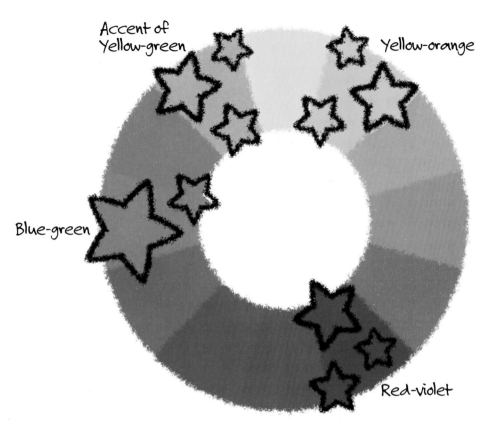

Accent of Yellow-green

Yellow-orange

Blue-green

Red-violet

Colors on a Triangle with an Accent

The balanced and satisfying colors in a triangle harmony can be made even more exciting by the addition of a fourth, or accent, color. It is easy to select an accent for this triangle color harmony. First, choose one of the colors in the triangle. Then, move directly across the color wheel to identify its opposite, or complement. Because there are three colors in the basic harmony, there will always be three possible choices for the accent color.

Accents are a good way to add a touch of unexpected color to an otherwise predictable color scheme. They are also a comfortable way to introduce a color you might not ordinarily choose, making your quilts more interesting, more unusual, and more satisfying because of the challenge presented by a new color.

Choose three colors on a triangle, then move directly across the color wheel from one of the three chosen colors to identify its opposite for the accent.

The quilt Autumn Glow began with three colors on a triangle—yellow-orange, blue-green, and red-violet. In this design, the red-based color plays the dominant role in the center medallion. Yellow-green, the opposite of the dominant color, serves as an understudy, but a very exciting one nonetheless. In the medallion, yellow-green adds an extra sparkle to the overall scheme. The two remaining colors on the triangle are also used in lesser proportions but still add eye-catching appeal to the center design.

Even though the color combinations available in this harmony may at first seem odd and difficult to combine, try replacing the pure colors with tints, tones, and shades to achieve the mood you're after. A multicolor print that stays true to the harmony may be the crowning touch.

Orange, green, violet, accent of blue

Color Options Within This Harmony

Yellow, blue, red, accent of green

Yellow-orange, blue-green, red-violet, accent of red-orange

Artificial dyes were accidentally discovered in 1856 by William Perkin as he was attempting to make synthetic quinine. Unfortunately, these first dyes completely faded away within ten years, but the era of artificial dyes had begun.

Yellow-green, red-orange, blue-violet, accent of yellow-orange

Crayonbox Memories

To a child, the color of winter is pure white snow, bright green mittens, brown woolen hats, big black boots, and icy blue winds. It is forest green pine trees, rosy pink cheeks, golden apple cider, and speedy red sleds. Many of my fondest memories of color are from the beautiful season of winter.

Ann

114

Multicolor Harmonies

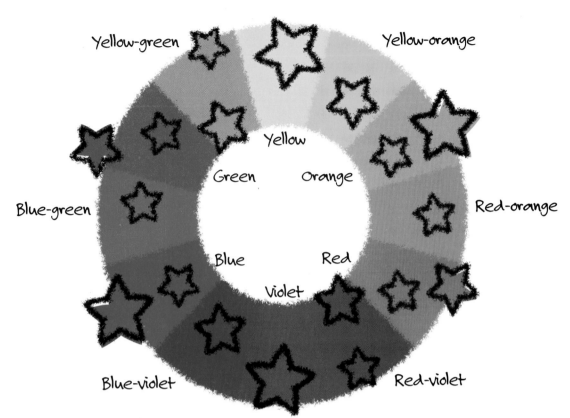

Yellow-green

Yellow-orange

Yellow

Green   Orange

Blue-green

Red-orange

Blue

Red

Violet

Blue-violet

Red-violet

M u l t i c o l o r   H a r m o n i e s

Many Colors

Some of the most visually exciting quilts are those made from many colors. The technical term for this harmony is *polychromatic*, which comes from the Greek words *poly* (meaning many) and *chroma* (meaning color). Just as the name implies, this uninhibited harmony allows you to use a wide variety of colors, in all of their varying tints and shades, to create a "quilt of many colors." When the harmony is stretched to include all of the colors of the spectrum, the scheme can be called the rainbow harmony.

Harmonies using many colors tend to be bright and uplifting. Because they span such a wide range on the color wheel, they usually include a pleasing mix of both cool and warm colors. The colors all work together, with no one color more important than the rest.

Choose a wide variety of colors, in all of their varying tints and shades.

A great deal of folk art, native costuming, and even stained glass work employ this color-rich harmony to great advantage. But to quilters, the Many Colors harmony is perhaps best exemplified by the familiar scrap quilt. It appears in the truly spontaneous utility quilts of the nineteenth century, constructed from whatever colorful bits and pieces tumbled from the scrap bag. It is equally apparent in the more carefully planned colorwash style, as seen in the quilt Garden Maze.

This is not to say that all quilts made using the Many Colors harmony must be scrap quilts. Many multicolored or rainbow quilts are made from a limited number of fabrics, perhaps two or three in each color family. As long as the color scheme covers a wide range on the color wheel, the quilt may still be called polychromatic.

MANY COLORS

Many colors

Color Options Within This Harmony

Many colors

Challenge yourself to use a new harmony for every quilt you plan. You'll become more comfortable combining colors you wouldn't ordinarily use, you'll explore paler and deeper shades of your favorite colors, and you'll expand your fabric collection to boot! Truly magical!

Crayonbox Memories

My brother, Wayne, and I were so close in age that we were often mistaken for twins. We learned early on that "twins" received more attention and more free candy samples from store clerks than regular ol' brother and sister shoppers. Whenever Mom shopped in the local five-and-dime, Wayne and I would casually glance toward the candy clerks, with me batting my eyelashes and Wayne smiling in his bashful way, because we knew it usually meant a treat for both of us.

My favorite goodie was a candy ice cream cone topped with marshmallow cream and just the right amount of stickiness. These mile-high marshmallow puffs were swirled with the yummiest shades of strawberry, lemon, and lime, and I always loved to pick out the cones with the largest dollop of goo. Of course, I had other favorites, too, like all-day suckers and sugary bubble gum. Suckers came in all colors and flavors, but the red ones just seemed to taste better, even though they didn't last any longer than the green or yellow treats. And, much to Mom's dismay, if pink bubble gum came my way, I could chew the same piece for days and it never lost its appeal.

An old-fashioned candy counter can still entice sweet-toothed kiddies into pressing their noses to the glass for a peek at the sugary confections on display. Perhaps today's youngsters could learn a trick or two from candy-tasting pros like us—flash a shy smile, hide behind Mom's skirt, and think sweet thoughts of colorful treats.

Joyce

119

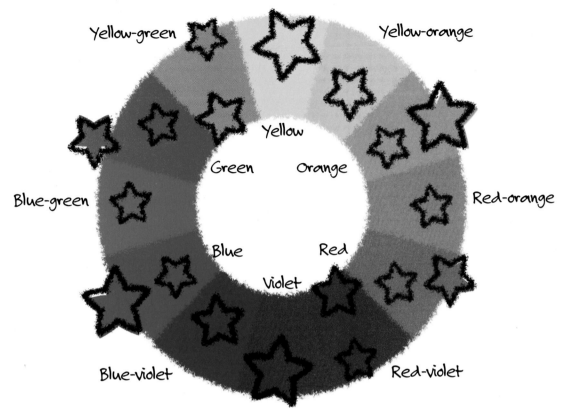

Yellow-green

Yellow-orange

Yellow

Green

Orange

Blue-green

Red-orange

Blue

Red

Violet

Blue-violet

Red-violet

Multicolor Harmonies

Main Color with Many Colors

Sometimes working with a Many Colors harmony can seem a bit overwhelming and chaotic, especially when working with scrap fabrics. With so many colors to manage, it is easy to feel the quilt slipping out of control. To give the design more focus, simply choose one color to play a more important role in the overall color scheme. The technical name, *polychromatic with dominant color*, might seem rather intimidating. So to make this final entry more user-friendly, call it a Main Color with Many Colors harmony.

> Use many colors, choosing one color as the main, and most-used, color.

By choosing a single color to play a more dominant role, you create a sense of unity in your quilt while still allowing the creative freedom of a wide variety of colors, textures, and prints. To understand how this harmony works, imagine your favorite garden and the multicolored blooms coexisting beautifully with their rich green foliage. The flowers cover a wide range of colors, but the common greenery creates a sense of peace and continuity. The same principle applies when a "walkway" of green hexagons is used to connect the blocks of a 1930s Grandmother's Flower Garden quilt!

The main color can be introduced subtly into the design as a background or be given a more obvious role by using it for setting squares and triangles, sashing, or borders. In the quilt Pathways, the main color green serves as a constant in the multicolored, scrappy blocks and is used for both the light and dark portions in the quilt. To complete the harmony, many colors around the color wheel were used in each block and work together to create a virtual rainbow of color.

Color Options Within This Harmony

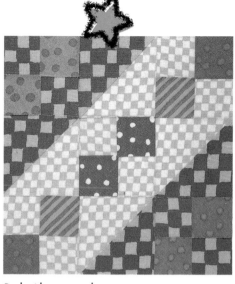

Red with many colors

Yellow-orange with many colors

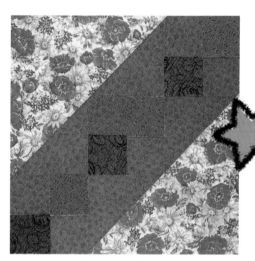

Red-orange with many colors

This is a fun block to use if you have a large-scale print that you've fallen in love with at your local quilt shop. To showcase your favorite fabric, cut a large triangle for the area outside the pathway and eliminate the two Four Patch corner blocks and the triangles on either side of them.

Orange with many colors

Yellow with many colors

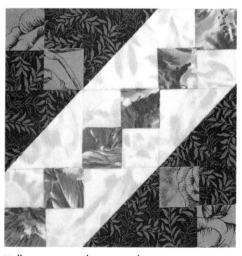

Yellow-green with many colors

Green with many colors

Blue-violet with many colors

Blue-green with many colors

Contrast is essential to the success of the Railroad block. Whether it is color contrast, value contrast, scale contrast, or temperature contrast, be sure each fabric you choose is distinctive and readable when placed next to the other fabrics, or your block will read as a single square of a jumbled multicolored print.

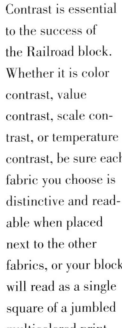

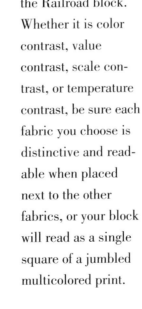

Blue with many colors

Violet with many colors

Red-violet with many colors

COLOR WORKSHOP

Explore the world of color by learning more about the magical effect of fabric—from value and texture to mood and harmony.

From the Color Wheel to Fabric

The best part of quiltmaking is fabric! Do you often feel the need to caress the luscious colors even though you know fabric is flat and two-dimensional? It's as if there were something you needed to absorb through touch that your eyes alone couldn't appreciate. Well, there is something drawing you in. It's visual texture, mood, and lightness and darkness. It's pattern, theme, and dimension. And each of these is as important to the study of color as actual color. Come into the Color Workshop, where you'll take the colors of the rainbow and translate them into fabric. The workshop door is open wide and a world of quiltmaking magic awaits you.

Red

Red is provocative and fiery and stimulates the emotions in a way few other colors do. It is the color of love and devotion. Red is creation, excitement, and blood—the most powerful life-giving force. When life is taken, red represents suffering. Red can be noble and lofty, yet it can symbolize charity and compassion. When it's tinted to pink, it gives way to sensuality and romance; when shaded to burgundy, it represents refinement and wealth.

Green

Green is natural and hopeful and represents a return to the earth. It symbolizes vegetation, cultivation, fertility, and fruitfulness. Green stirs the emotions with thoughts of reliance, trust, and understanding. In mournful times, it can be sympathetic, and in times of discord, it can be empathetic. Green is adaptable, caring, and giving. As green lightens in intensity, mellow earthiness is replaced by crisp, cool images. When green darkens, it often becomes more powerful and drama-filled.

Violet

Violet is rich, lush, and vibrant. Like royalty, it can
have intellect, dignity, and power, but violet can also be
passive, like majestic mountains seen from afar. It evokes
a spiritual, ethereal quality and borders on the sublime.
Violet can be construed as demanding by many; it is an
equal mix of the calm nature of blue and the passion of
red, creating a struggle for position. Light violets are
pleasant yet cool, while dark violets are
thought-provoking and somber.

Yellow

Yellow is brilliant and bright and shines like the light of the sun. Its warmth radiates, dazzles, and illuminates everything close to it. Yellow can add life, intelligence, intuition, and reason, but it can also overwhelm, upset, and cause the senses to lessen its impact. When lightened, yellow is soft, cheery, and pleasant; when darkened to gold, it represents another wave of human responses—glory, adoration, and praise.

Blue

Blue, the age-old friend, is devoted and true. It is the color of the heavens and the seas. Blue represents the traits of knowledge and innocence and conveys a sense of peace, relaxation, and stillness. It is halfway between black and white, giving it equilibrium and poise. Blue is darkness made visible. Lighten it with white to create a mood that's cool or cold; darken it with black to stir up blue's stormy mysterious side.

Orange

Orange is proud, ambitious, arrogant, and conceited.
Its strength lies in the often-negative reaction it causes.
Orange may convey ominous, forbidding, even menacing
meanings. It is also a color of buffoonery and clowning. Is
it any wonder that orange is associated with Halloween,
the holiday of pranks, mischief, and the netherworld?
Once orange softens to peach, the melodrama disappears,
and a feeling of acceptance and warmth comes forth.
As orange darkens into brown, it becomes quiet
and restful, sad and wistful, like
rustling leaves in autumn.

The Importance of LIGHTS, MEDIUMS, and DARKS

Sometimes the difference between a nice safe quilt design and a unique, exciting one is a simple change in the placement of the light, medium, and dark fabrics. Most quilt blocks need an interplay of all of these values to be successful.

It is nearly impossible to visualize how a block will change when the lights, mediums, and darks switch positions. But it is a very simple process to work out on paper. The process, called grayscaling, requires only paper and a pencil; ¼-inch graph paper works best. Draft small versions of your block, then shade it a variety of ways. Make the background recede by penciling in

darks in the outer areas, or make the points pop with a light. Blend an interior area by using a mix of mediums. Or create a focal point in the center of a block by using high-contrast lights and darks next to each other.

Be sure to "combine" neighboring patchwork areas into one larger unit, assigning them the same value to see how dramatic the block is when the elements have changed "shape." Keep experimenting until you create a look you love for your quilt. Taking time at this stage in the quilt-planning process can uncover unexpected effects and a magical block design!

Make the block center the focal point

Create diagonal movement by aligning the darks

Play up outer triangles to create a star

Identifying VALUE in Fabric

Most quilters rely heavily on mediums

Lights

Use light fabrics in your quilt to present a look that's airy and delicate. Light-value prints and solids are ideal for backgrounds. When used in large numbers, light tints have a gossamer, fairy-tale quality. If you want your quilting stitches to play a major role, choose light fabrics for the areas that will be heavily quilted.

Mediums

Medium-value fabrics are the easiest fabrics to find and use. They are "safe" in any design and certainly noncontroversial. You may be drawn to mediums because they are pleasing to the eye, but be sure to balance them with lights and darks or the resulting quilt will be flat and uninspiring.

Use lights and darks to create high contrast

Darks

Dark fabrics add weight and depth to a quilt, and they can influence the shapes we see in a design because they usually advance. Almost every quilt can benefit from the addition of a dark or two, even if only in small amounts. Very deep darks can make the light-value fabrics seem even brighter and add an almost-twinkling impression.

133

The Difference between SOLIDS and PRINTS

You can read stacks of books on color theory, admire hundreds of finished quilts, then purchase a trunkful of colorful fabric. But until you actually try the color harmonies you've studied and practiced with real fabric, you may never experience the joy of combining colors that harmonize.

A good way to move from color theory to actual fabric is to take your color wheel and a list of the different color harmonies to the quilt shop and experiment with some of your new color knowledge. On this trip, use your time to relax, explore, and discover the exciting world of color. Using bolts of solid-color fabric, pull together the colors for one or two harmonies. Once you have a color harmony arranged, begin to substitute print fabrics for the solid colors.

While solid-color fabrics tend to be harmonious in almost any combination, print fabrics are trickier to use. They contain more than one color, and the print size and style can impact the look of your chosen palette.

Once you've replaced all of the solids with prints, evaluate your selections. If you've chosen too many busy prints, change one of them to a tone-on-tone or hand-dyed fabric to calm the mix. If your pile of bolts seems uninspiring, add darker or lighter fabrics. If the prints blend and become indistinguishable, try a large-scale print to add interest. Be adventurous and use the more unusual or "larger" harmonies. You'll find that some of the oddest color combinations make the most incredible quilts.

MOVING from Design to Fabric

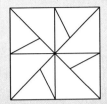

Learning about value and color is important, but the thrill of fabric can't be beat! It's time to transform a block from a black-and-white drawing to a block mockup of actual fabrics. Many quilters use colored pencils to test colors, but the only real representation of fabric color is fabric itself. Making a block mockup is easy. Choose a block and sample fabrics, then cut the fabrics to fit the areas of the blocks. Keep changing the look of your block by changing or rearranging fabrics.

Either copy one of the blocks from this book or draft your chosen block, then photocopy it several times. If possible, make one copy on card stock, or redraft the block on the heavier stock to use for the mockup. On one copy of your block, place an ✕ in

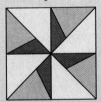

each patchwork piece to indicate the right side, then cut the pieces apart and set them aside. Using the remaining photocopies and a pencil, grayscale the block in a variety of ways; see page 132.

Select about 20 fabrics using any harmony, including at least three fabrics in each value you've grayscaled. Then, using the grayscaling as a guideline for value placement, use a glue stick to glue the right side of the paper pieces to the wrong side of a few fabrics. Trim the fabrics along the paper edge, but do not remove the papers.

Place the fabric pieces on the mockup block following the outlines. Try different values and colors in the same place either by peeling the unwanted fabric off the paper and replacing it or by gluing a new fabric piece on top of an old one. Perfection is not required! This

process is trial and error, so continue changing fabrics until you are satisfied with your block. Glue the fabrics in place.

Make your mockups with the fabrics you have on hand. Concern yourself only with getting the color correct; don't worry about including particular fabrics. Your finished mockup can become the basis for planning the rest of your quilt.

Understanding Visual

TEXTURE

The visual texture of a fabric is as important as its color. Each fabric you choose has a style that defines the way it looks or the type of visual texture it has. Since fabric is two-dimensional, quilt blocks benefit from a pleasing mix of print styles. Imagine a quilt block using only tiny calicoes in medium-value pinks and blues. How boring! Visual texture is a way of adding ZING to a block.

There are many categories of visual texture in fabric and you probably have most of them in your stash already. Directional, large-scale, representational, and allover prints are just a few of the most popular texture prints available. Hand-dyed fabrics and soft "sueded" cottons are visual texture newcomers but can dramatically improve a block that suffers from the "blahs."

Geometrics

Color Harmony: Three Side-by-Side Colors
Colors Used: Red, red-orange, orange

Geometrics are abstract and contemporary. They are based on geometric figures, like dots, triangles, circles, squares, and other fun shapes and are usually allover prints. You can skillfully combine geometrics in a single block, or use them singly to add interest to other visual textures.

Florals

Color Harmony: Main Color
with Many Colors
Colors Used: Yellow-green
with many colors

Flowers have always been the most popular subject for printed fabric. Small florals are traditionally known as calicoes. Large florals can give a sense of movement to a block when cut apart for smaller patchwork pieces or can add an elegant touch to a wide border.

Plaids and Checks

Color Harmony: Two Colors and Their Opposites
Colors Used: Red, green, blue, orange

Plaids and checks add a country feeling to a quilt. The fabrics are usually woven rather than printed. Don't worry about cutting plaids and checks exactly on-grain; cut slightly off-grain or on the diagonal, they'll add movement and variety to a block. Have fun combining several plaids and checks to create a scrappy casual look.

Tone on Tones

Color Harmony: Opposite Colors
Colors Used: Yellow, violet

Tone on tones are also known as one-color fabrics. They have texture yet appear solid when viewed from a short distance. These fabrics are more interesting than plain solids because they add a subtle amount of visual texture. Tone-on-tone fabrics are especially useful as background fabrics and in areas where you want to show off elaborate quilting stitches.

Stripes

Color Harmony: Every Other Color
Colors Used: Red, orange, yellow, green, blue, violet

Stripes come in all widths and styles, from straight and narrow to wide and wavy. Border prints are really just another style of stripe. You can use stripes to direct the viewer's eye and create movement. If stripes are used as a border fabric, consider mitering the corners so the stripe flows continuously around the quilt.

Recognizing Color Harmonies in MULTICOLOR Fabrics

Unless you weave and dye your own fabric (and who has time when there are quilts to make?), you must rely on the current offerings of the fabric manufacturers. Multicolor fabrics are a great starting point when planning a color scheme for a quilt. If you can recognize a harmony in the color print, picking the other fabrics for the quilt will be simple.

First, choose a fabric that you'd really like to work with and jot down all of the colors you see in it. Remember to think about all 12 colors on the color wheel. Next, page through the Color Harmonies chapter and try to find a harmony that closely matches the multicolor fabric you've chosen.

Sometimes there may be a small amount of a color in the fabric that isn't a part of the harmony. Just ignore it because it will not affect your project. You may also find a print that has many of the colors of a particular harmony, but not all of them. Don't despair! All you need to do is add those colors as part of your total fabric selection.

The multicolor print you choose may not have the colors in the same proportions you wish to use—include the fabric anyway. Just adjust the color amounts according to your tastes and needs. You'll be amazed at how easy this process is and how much confidence you'll gain when selecting fabrics.

Color Harmony: Three Side-by-Side Colors

Colors Used: Red-orange, orange, yellow-orange

Color Harmony: Two Colors Separated by One Color

Colors Used: Yellow-green, blue-green

Color Harmony: Two Colors Separated by Three Colors

Colors Used: Red, yellow

Color Harmony: Two Colors and Their Opposites

Colors Used: Red, green, yellow, violet

Color Harmony: Three Alternating Colors

Colors Used: Green, violet, blue

Color Harmony: Many Colors

Colors Used: Many colors

Change the MOOD by Changing the Fabric

Have you ever found a block you love in a color scheme you didn't like? It's easy to transform that basic block into a theme and palette that inspire you. Decide which mood you would like to create, select a color harmony, then work with a color option in the harmony that has the look you want. Finding print fabrics that illustrate your theme is the finishing touch!

Crayonbox Colors

Color Harmony:
Every Other Color

Colors Used:
Red, orange, yellow, green, blue, violet

It's bright and bold, and kids will love it! Combine color wheel colors with a wacky geometric print to create a block that is just plain fun.

Lullaby Time

Color Harmony:
Two Colors Separated by Three Colors

Colors Used: Blue, red

Forget fabrics printed with playful rattles, diaper pins, and baby bottles! Baby's first quilt can use cute-as-a-button prints in soft pink and blue to say "I love you."

Springtime Florals

Color Harmony:
Opposite Colors with an Accent

Colors Used:
Violet, yellow, accent of green

Be inspired by the fresh blooms of spring and create a block full of eye-catching color. Search for floral prints of tulips and daffodils to round out your theme.

Country Homespun

Color Harmony:
Two Colors and Their Opposites

Colors Used:
Red, green, blue, orange

Small prints, checks, stripes, and stars give this block the look of a bygone era. Use shirting-style prints or reproduction fabrics for a darker, more masculine theme.

Patriotic Salute

Color Harmony:
Two Colors Separated by Three Colors

Colors Used:
Blue, red

Hooray for the red, white, and blue! Like firecrackers on the 4th of July, bright star-studded prints come in all styles and sizes for year-round patriotic celebrations.

BLOCK
Makeovers

It's easy to create a block you like, but it's hard to challenge yourself to change any of the fabrics in that block once you're comfortable with the look you've created. Oftentimes, however, a single fabric or fabric value change can turn a good block into a great block.

After you've made a sample block, step back from your work and analyze your choices. Do all the block elements stand out or do they seem to blend together? Have you chosen fabrics with different-size prints? Do your fabrics create a unified mood or compete with one another?

View your block objectively. You may need to substitute a fabric you adore with one you're less enthusiastic about, especially if the change makes the block more successful. Adding fabrics with interesting prints, textures, and moods can transform a nice block design into a showstopper.

Print Sizes Too Similar

Vary the scale of the printed fabrics

Good

Better

Quilters rely heavily on fabrics in the medium-scale print range. But it's important to vary the scale, or size, of the printed motifs you use. The good block is successful, but look at what happened when we added a small-scale print to the Four Patch blocks. Magic! The small-scale print makes the fabrics distinguishable from one another. A darker and smaller-scale print adds depth to the center "pathway."

Color Harmony: Two Colors Separated by One Color

Colors Used: Blue-violet, red-violet

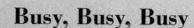

Busy, Busy, Busy

Use tone-on-tones to avoid busyness

Good

Better

While visual texture is important, too many prints together will overwhelm the block. In the good block, each print tries to be the center of attention. In the better block, we replaced the dark green and red-violet prints, using tone-on-tones to create a calmer design. This allowed the star-within-a-square to become the focus.

Color Harmony: Two Colors and Their Opposites

Colors Used: Red-violet, yellow-green, red-orange, blue-green

A Case of the Doldrums

Add excitement with peppier prints

Good   **Better**

Variety is the spice of life! The good block features a pleasing mix of country prints and could be described as a nice safe block. But imagine making this same block 60 times for a bed-size quilt—what monotony! In the better block, we added a darker (and more exciting) red check that forms a secondary pinwheel to accentuate the spinning motion.

Color Harmony: Two Colors Separated by Three Colors

Colors Used: Blue, red

Find prints that reflect the quilt's theme

Conflicting Moods

Good   **Better**

A block's success can also depend on the mood it creates. When selecting fabrics, it's important to focus on a theme and choose prints that reflect that theme. While the good block was bright and fun, the sailboat look was interrupted with a uniformly printed geometric fabric. In the better block, we substituted a wave-and-water print to keep the sailing mood light and lively.

Color Harmony: Three Side-by-Side Colors

Colors Used: Blue-green, blue, blue-violet

Change a few mediums to lights and darks

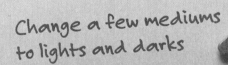

Not Enough Contrast

Good   **Better**

One of the most common pitfalls when designing and planning a quilt is using too many medium-value fabrics. In the good block, the mediums seem to meld in the center of the block since they are placed next to each other. In the better block, we added a second, darker red fabric and a lighter, brighter orange print to create crisp lines that more clearly define the block's elements.

Color Harmony: Opposite Colors with an Accent

Colors Used: Red, green, accent of orange

COLORFUL QUILTS

Rev up the sewing machine, put a spin on the spools, and apply the harmonies of color to your next quilt project.

Butterflies Are Free

This Japanese butterfly print perfectly illustrates the color harmony Opposite Colors with an Accent. With a soft blue-violet for a background, the lively yellow-orange butterflies complement the surrounding fabric and add excitement. The dash of red-orange color in the wings and sashing becomes the accent for this harmony and rounds out a three-color combination that can't be beat.

Harmony Featured

Opposite Colors with an Accent

Colors Used

Blue-violet, yellow-orange, accent of red-orange

MATERIALS

¼ yard large-scale blue-violet print

⅜ yard light blue-violet print

⅛ yard dark blue-violet print

⅛ yard medium blue-violet print

⅛ yard yellow-orange print

⅛ yard red-orange print

⅜ yard gray print

⅜ yard backing fabric

⅜ yard binding fabric

24-inch square of quilt batting

Assorted crystal seed beads and metallic bugle beads

SKILL LEVEL: INTERMEDIATE

Finished Quilt Size: 20¼" square

Finished Block Size: 7½"

Number of Blocks: 4

Magical Beginnings

Find a wonderful large-scale fabric or picture print you love and showcase it in the center of these blocks. You could highlight different areas of the fabric or you could cut all four centers with the same motif. A variation of the Crown of Thorns pattern, this block uses both fast-and-easy rotary cutting methods and a simple template. You will need to make a template for pattern piece A on page 150; for information about making and using templates, see page 247.

CUTTING

All measurements include a ¼-inch seam allowance. Referring to the chart, cut the required number of strips and patches for your quilt. Some strips are only cut once, so no additional cutting information will appear in the second or third columns. Cut all strips across the crosswise grain or fabric width. Read "Making a Window Template" on the opposite page before cutting the block centers. **Note:** Cut and piece one sample block before cutting all of the fabric for the quilt.

C U T T I N G

FABRIC	Used For	First Cut		Second Cut			Third Cut	
		Strip Width	No. to Cut	Shape	Dimensions	No. to Cut	Shape	Total No. Needed
Large-scale blue-violet print	Block centers	3½"*	1	▢	3½" × 3½"	4	—	—
Light blue-violet print	Quarter-triangle squares	2¾"	1	▢	2¾" × 2¾"	4	—	—
	Borders	2½"	3	—	—	—	—	—
	Large triangles	2⅜"	1	▢	2⅜" × 2⅜"	8	◨	16
Medium blue-violet print	A	A pieces	16	—	—	—	—	—
Dark blue-violet print	Triangle squares	2⅜"	1	■	2⅜" × 2⅜"	16	—	—
Yellow-orange print	Quarter-triangle squares	2¾"	1	▢	2¾" × 2¾"	8	—	—
Red-orange print	Vertical sashing	¾"	2	▭	¾" × 8"	6	—	—
	Horizontal sashing	¾"	2	▭	¾" × 16¼"	3	—	—
Gray print	Squares	2"	1	▢	2" × 2"	16	—	—
	Triangle squares	2⅜"	1	▢	2⅜" × 2⅜"	16	—	—
	Quarter-triangle squares	2¾"	1	▢	2¾" × 2¾"	4	—	—
Binding fabric	Binding	2½"	3	—	—	—	—	—

*If using a picture print, see "Making a Window Template" on the opposite page.

Making a Window Template

Try using a window template to view large-scale prints for the block centers in this quilt. If you don't have a purchased one, make your own! Cut a 6-inch square from graph paper, then cut a 3½-inch opening in the center of the square.

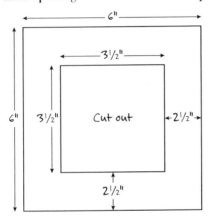

Place the "window" over the selected fabric to get a quick look at how your chosen motif will look in the finished block. Remember that ¼ inch all around will become the seam allowance, so make adjustments in your positioning as necessary. The large graph paper border around the opening helps to visually isolate the motif from the surrounding fabric.

Once you're ready to cut the patches for your quilt, you may want to paste the graph paper template to card stock or template plastic for durability. Center the "window" on your selected motif, then use a pencil or quilt marker to mark the opening on your fabric. The drawn lines will be the cutting lines for the 3½-inch center square.

PIECING THE BLOCKS

1. With right sides together, center and sew an A piece to the top and bottom of the block center, pressing the seam toward A. In the same manner, center and sew an A piece to each side of the block center, as shown in **Diagram 1.**

Diagram 1

2. With right sides together, center and sew a large light blue-violet triangle to opposite sides of the block. Press the seams toward the triangles.

In the same manner, sew triangles to each of the remaining sides, as shown in **Diagram 2.**

Diagram 2

3. To make a triangle square, layer a 2⅜-inch gray square and a same-size dark blue-violet square right sides together. Draw a diagonal line across the top square, taking care not to stretch the fabric, then sew ¼ inch to either side of the drawn line. Using a rotary cutter, cut the square in half on the drawn line. Press the triangle square open, pressing the seam toward the dark blue-violet fabric. See **Diagram 3**. Repeat to make a total of 32 triangle squares.

Diagram 3

4. Layer a 2¾-inch yellow-orange square and a same-size gray square right sides together, with the yellow-orange square on top. Referring to **Diagram 4**, draw an X from corner to corner on the top square, taking care not to stretch the fabric. Sew ¼ inch from the drawn lines. Using a rotary cutter, cut apart on the drawn lines. Press the seams toward the gray. Repeat to make a total of 16 pieced triangles.

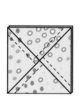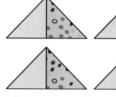

Diagram 4

5. With right sides together, layer a 2¾-inch yellow-orange square and a same-size light blue-violet square and repeat the process in Step 4. Press the seam toward the light blue-violet. Repeat to make a total of 16 pieced triangles.

6. With right sides together, match and sew the center seams of a yellow-orange/gray triangle and a yellow-orange/light blue-violet triangle to make a quarter-triangle square, as shown in **Diagram 5**. Press the seam to one side. Repeat to make a total of 16 quarter-triangle squares.

Diagram 5

7. Sew one triangle square to each side of a quarter-triangle square, as shown in **Diagram 6**. Be sure the triangle-square seams are oriented correctly. Press the seams toward the triangle squares. Repeat to make a total of 16 units.

Diagram 6

8. With right sides together, sew one of these units to each side of the block, carefully matching the seams of the side units with the seams at the center of the block. See **Diagram 7**. Press the seams toward the center.

Diagram 7

9. With right sides together, sew one 2-inch gray square to each side of the remaining units for the top and bottom, as shown in **Diagram 8**. Press the seams toward the gray squares. Repeat to make a total of eight units.

Diagram 8

10. With right sides together, sew one unit to the top and bottom of the block, as shown in **Diagram 9**. Be sure to match the seams at the top and bottom units with the seams at the center of the block. Press the seams toward the center. Repeat to make a total of four blocks.

Diagram 9

ASSEMBLING THE QUILT

1. Use a flat surface to arrange the blocks, vertical sashing strips, and horizontal sashing strips, as shown in the **Assembly Diagram.**

2. With right sides together, sew the rows of vertical sashing strips and blocks to each other. To add a sashing strip, fold it in half crosswise and crease. Unfold it and position it right side down along the side of the first block, matching the crease to the horizontal center of the block. Pin at the midpoint and ends, and place additional pins along the length as necessary, easing in any fullness. Sew the sashing to the block. Press the seam toward the sashing. Repeat for all of the blocks and vertical sashing strips.

3. Sew the horizontal sashing to the block rows. Fold the first horizontal sashing strip in half crosswise and crease. Repeat for the first row of blocks. Match the midpoints, pinning at the center and ends first, then along the length of the entire sashing strip, easing in any fullness. Sew the sashing strip to the row, then press the seam toward the sashing. Repeat for the remaining two sashing strips.

Assembly Diagram

ADDING THE BORDERS

1. Attach the top and bottom borders first. Measure the width of the quilt top, taking the measurement through the horizontal center of the quilt, rather than along the edges. Cut two border strips this exact length.

2. Fold one strip in half crosswise and crease. Unfold it and position it right side down along the top of the quilt, with the crease at the vertical midpoint. Pin at the midpoint and ends first, then along the length of the entire edge, easing in any fullness. Sew the border to the quilt. Repeat for the bottom border. Press the seams toward the borders.

3. Measure the length of the quilt top, taking the measurement through the vertical center of the quilt and including the top and bottom borders. Cut two border strips this exact length and sew these to the sides of the quilt, referring to Step 2. Press the seams toward the borders.

HINTS FROM HAZEL

Always wash and press your fabrics to remove stiffness and sizing before using them. Try washing your yardage as soon as you arrive home from the fabric store. Then press it and fold it carefully for storage. Avoid storing fabric in paper bags because of the high acid content or in plastic bags because of trapped moisture; both of these can break down cotton fibers or stain fabric. If you prepare your fabrics for sewing as soon as you buy them, you'll always be ready to cut, sew, and go!

QUILTING AND FINISHING

1. Mark the quilt top for quilting. The blocks and sashing in this quilt were quilted in the ditch. The butterflies in the large-scale print were quilted along their outlines. Short curved lines were quilted in the borders.

2. Cut a 24-inch square of backing fabric.

3. Layer the quilt top, batting, and backing and baste the layers together. Quilt as desired.

4. Make double-fold binding and sew it to the quilt, following the directions on page 250.

Happy Endings

Add a sparkling touch to your large-scale print with crystal seed beads or metallic bugle beads. Use a slim beading needle or a hand-sewing needle with a small eye and matching thread to attach the beads. Think creatively when deciding where to place the beads. You could outline a printed shape or create a new one with the beads. Or sew the beads where sunlight would naturally glisten, like on a butterfly's wing or antenna. Take care to keep your stitches buried between the layers of the quilt so that they won't show on the back.

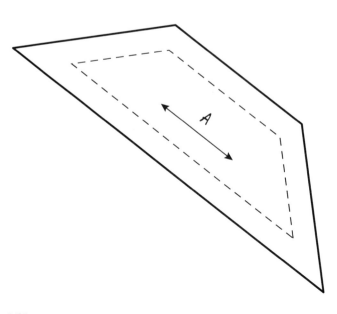

150

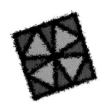

SpinWheels

The variety of color that can be obtained with just yellow-orange and yellow-green fabrics is amazing, and that's what the harmony Two Colors Separated by One Color sets out to prove. While some fabrics are mostly orange and others are predominantly green, as a collection, they are unified by the color they have in common—yellow. When selecting fabrics for a quilt like SpinWheels, don't ignore the uglies! Since your color choices can enhance the movement of the pinwheel shapes, often-overlooked garish prints can turn these traditional pinwheels into spinwheels of unforgettable color.

Harmony Featured

Two Colors Separated by One Color

Colors Used

Yellow-orange and yellow-green

MATERIALS

⅝ yard large yellow-orange print

⅛ yard each of 22 yellow-orange prints

⅛ yard each of 28 yellow-green prints

¼ yard very dark brown print

1 yard backing fabric

⅜ yard binding fabric

36-inch square of quilt batting

SKILL LEVEL: EASY

Finished Quilt Size: 31¾" square

Finished Block Size: 4¾"

Number of Blocks: 25

Magical Beginnings

To re-create the scrappy look of this quilt, use as many yellow-orange and yellow-green fabrics as you can find. If you plan to use each fabric just one time, you will need a total of 50 different fabrics for the blocks. This quilt contains 22 yellow-orange fabrics and 28 yellow-green fabrics, and the directions reflect this ratio. Feel free, however, to change these amounts and proportions. Since you only need a small amount of most fabrics, it may be easier and more cost-effective to buy fat quarters (18 × 20-inch rectangles) for greater variety. Or dig deep into your scrap bag for bits and pieces of your chosen colors.

The blocks in this quilt are paper pieced, so you will need to prepare two paper foundations for each block, using the **Block Pattern** on page 157. For information on preparing foundations and paper piecing, refer to page 248.

It's best to choose the border fabric after the blocks are assembled. Depending on the block placement, your border may need to tone down the colors or unify them. All seam allowances are ¼ inch unless specified otherwise.

CUTTING

Refer to the chart below, and cut the required number of strips and pieces. The cut sizes of the fabric strips include generous seam allowances. With the foundation method, it's easier to work with wider strips, especially when you are paper piecing triangles. You may wish to decrease the width of the strips by ⅛-inch increments as you become more familiar with this technique. Cut all strips across the crosswise grain, or fabric width. **Note:** Cut and piece one sample block on a foundation before cutting all the fabric for the quilt.

PIECING THE BLOCKS

Each block contains two different fabrics—one fabric for the background and corners and another for the pinwheels; see the **Block Diagram** on page 154. In some instances, the blocks contain two yellow-green fabrics; in other blocks, there are two yellow-orange fabrics or a combination of a yellow-green and a yellow-orange fabric. Plan the layout for your quilt by combining various fabrics

C U T T I N G

FABRIC	Used For	First Cut Strip Width	First Cut No. to Cut	Second Cut Shape	Second Cut Dimensions	Second Cut No. to Cut	Third Cut Shape	Total No. Needed
Large yellow-orange print	Outer border	4"	4	—	—	—	—	—
Yellow-orange prints	Pinwheels	—	—	▭	3¼" × 5"	44	—	—
	Corners	—	—	▢	3¼" × 3¼"	24	◨	48
	Background*	—	—	▭	2¼" × 5"	48	—	—
Yellow-green prints	Pinwheels	—	—	▭	3¼" × 5"	56	—	—
	Corners	—	—	▢	3¼" × 3¼"	26	◨	52
	Background*	—	—	▭	2¼" × 5"	52	—	—
Very dark brown print	Inner border	1"	4	—	—	—	—	—
Binding fabric	Binding	2½"	4	—	—	—	—	—

*Cut the background from the same fabrics used for the corners.

with high, medium, and low contrast, then arrange them as shown in the **Assembly Diagram** on page 156 or as desired.

Block Diagram

HINTS FROM HAZEL

If you want each block in the quilt to make its own statement, create blocks that alternate lights and darks. The first block could have light fabric for the background, and the second block could have light fabric for the pinwheels. These should be set alternately for the best effect. Or set blocks with similar shading next to each other for a watercolor effect.

1. Fabric strips are positioned on the back, or unmarked, side of the foundation. Strips are added in numerical order starting at 1. All sewing takes place on the front side, directly on the drawn lines. All lines on the foundation, except the dashed one around the outer perimeter, are seam lines. To begin, layer a pinwheel piece on top of a background piece, with right sides together. Position these pieces underneath one of the paper piecing foundations, so that the pinwheel piece lies against the paper foundation, as shown in **Diagram 1.** The edges of the pieces must extend ¼ inch beyond the seam line between 1 and 2 on the paper foundation, as shown. Making 12 to 14 stitches per inch, sew on the line separating 1 and 2, beginning and ending the stitching at the dashed cutting lines, as shown.

2. Flip the background piece into a right-side-up position, pressing it firmly in place; see **Diagram 2.** Hold the foundation up to the light with the paper side toward you. You will now be able to see the shadow created by the background fabric. The shadow should overlap all lines drawn for the background piece. If it does not, use a seam ripper to remove the background from the foundation, then reposition the piece and try again. This ensures that there will be enough seam allowance on all sides when you add the adjacent fabric strips.

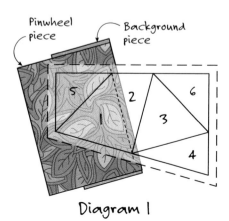

Pinwheel piece

Background piece

Diagram 1

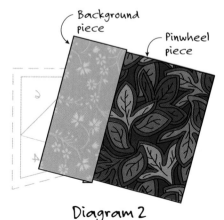

Background piece

Pinwheel piece

Diagram 2

3. Referring to **Diagram 3,** place a pinwheel piece right sides together with the 1 and 2 pieces. It may be helpful to pin the loose edges of pieces 1 and 2 to the foundation paper to avoid lumps when adding the next piece. Be sure the new pinwheel piece extends at least ¼ inch beyond the seam line between 2 and 3, then sew along this seam line.

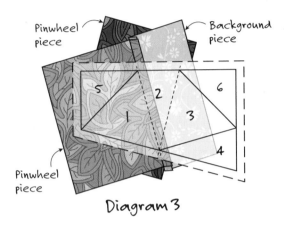

Diagram 3

4. Trim the background and pinwheel pieces to a scant ¼ inch beyond the seam line between 2 and 3, as shown in **Diagram 4;** be sure to fold the foundation paper away from the fabric to avoid cutting it as you trim the seam allowance. Flip the pinwheel piece into a right-side-up position, pressing it firmly in place.

Fold back
foundation paper, then trim here
Diagram 4

5. Add the next background piece to the foundation, in the same manner as the pinwheel piece in Step 3.

6. To make it easier to align the corner triangles, use a rotary cutter and ruler to trim around the block to remove excess fabric before adding the corners. Be sure to trim on the dashed line, not the solid line, of the foundation, as shown in **Diagram 5.**

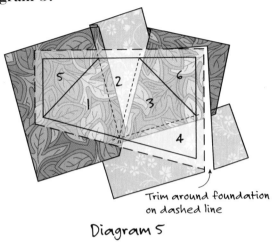

Trim around foundation
on dashed line
Diagram 5

7. To finish the corners, place a corner triangle right sides together with the pinwheel and sew the seam line between 1 and 5, as shown in **Diagram 6.** Trim the pinwheel fabric, then flip the triangle into a right-side-up position, pressing it firmly in place. Add the remaining corner in the same manner.

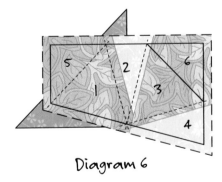

Diagram 6

8. Repeat Steps 1 through 7 to make the second half of the block. Use a rotary cutter and ruler to trim the excess fabric from the corners. With right sides of the fabric together, pin and sew the two halves of the block together, being sure to match center points, as shown in **Diagram 7** on page 156. Carefully remove the foundations.

155

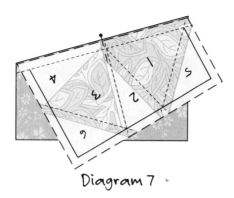

Diagram 7

9. Repeat Steps 1 through 8 to make 25 blocks total.

ASSEMBLING THE QUILT

1. Lay out the finished blocks in five rows of five blocks each, as shown in the **Assembly Diagram.**

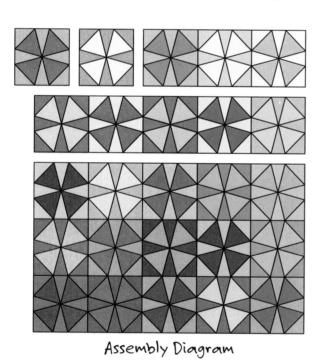

Assembly Diagram

2. With right sides together, sew the blocks together in horizontal rows; match seams carefully. Press seams in opposite directions from row to row.

Marking on Colorful Fabric

Marking quilting designs can be tricky until you find the best marking tool for the color of fabric you're quilting. Light solids and prints can be marked with a variety of pencils. Try a sharp #3 or #4 pencil for a very fine line, but be careful not to smudge it. Many quilters choose Berol Verithin pencils, available in white, yellow, and silver, for all of their marking needs, since they work on a variety of fabric colors. Dark fabrics can be marked with white charcoal pencils; the soft lead creates a fine line that can be partially removed with a simple brushing motion. The marks will disappear completely when rinsed out or washed.

Chalk products, such as chalk pencils, tailor's chalk, chalk wheels, and pouncers, are available in many colors and work on most lights, mediums, and darks, and prints and solids. The markings can be easily brushed away, so there's no need for washing. Soapstone markers were recently introduced and contain a narrow "lead" of soapstone that works best on medium and dark fabrics.

3. With right sides together, sew the rows of blocks together, matching seams carefully. Press the seam allowances toward the bottom edge of the quilt.

ADDING THE BORDERS

1. Attach the top and bottom inner borders first. Measure the width of the quilt top, taking the measurement through the horizontal center of the quilt. Cut two inner border strips this exact length.

2. Fold one of the inner border strips in half crosswise and crease. Unfold it and position it right side down along the top of the quilt, with the crease at the vertical midpoint. Pin at the midpoint and ends first, then along the length of the entire edge, easing in fullness as necessary. Sew the border to the quilt. Repeat for the bottom border. Press seams toward the borders.

3. Measure the length of the quilt, taking the measurement through the vertical center of the quilt and including the top and bottom borders. Cut two inner border strips this exact length.

4. Fold one strip in half crosswise and crease. Unfold it and position it right side down along one side of the quilt, with the crease at the horizontal midpoint. Pin at the midpoint and ends first, then along the length of the entire side, easing in fullness as necessary. Sew the border to the quilt top. Repeat on the opposite side of the quilt. Press seams toward the border.

5. Prepare and add the outer borders to the quilt in the same manner as for the inner borders, sewing on the top and bottom borders first, then the side borders.

QUILTING AND FINISHING

1. Mark quilting designs as desired. The blocks in this quilt were handquilted ¼ inch outside the pinwheel seam lines. Simple leaf shapes were joined end-to-end to form a chain-of-leaves design for the outer border. If you selected a border print with a definable motif, try echo quilting around the printed shapes.

2. Cut a 36-inch square of backing fabric.

3. Layer the quilt top, batting, and backing, and baste the layers together. Quilt as desired.

4. Make double-fold binding and sew it to the quilt, following the directions on page 250.

Happy Endings

The earthy shades of this quilt make it ideal for autumn. For fun, make similar quilts in winter, spring, and summer colors, then change your display when the seasons change. And, the best part is each quilt fits the same quilt hanger!

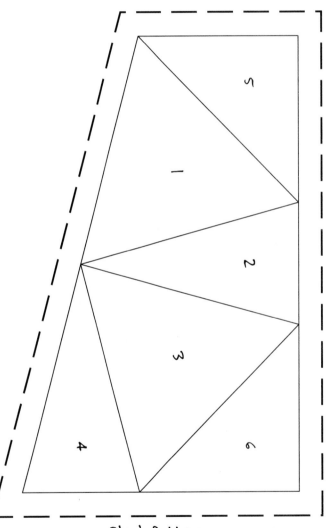

Block Pattern

When Stars Collide

Stars, meteors, and comets illuminate our nighttime sky with beautiful light and color. This wall quilt, with its fun futuristic look at the solar system, is based on the harmony Three Colors and Their Opposites. Using a total of six colors, the harmony is a perfect blend of warm and cool colors and represents the brightness of sunlight and the darkness of night.

Harmony Featured

Three Colors and Their Opposites

Colors Used

Violet, blue-violet, blue, yellow, yellow-orange, orange

MATERIALS

¾ yard total of violet, blue-violet, and blue prints

½ yard dark blue-violet print

¾ yard total of yellow, yellow-orange, and orange prints

⅛ yard yellow-orange print

⅞ yard backing fabric

⅜ yard binding fabric

28-inch square of quilt batting

SKILL LEVEL: ADVANCED

Finished Quilt Size: 24" square

Finished Block Size: 5½"

Number of Blocks: 9

Magical Beginnings

This quilt fools the eye. It looks as if it is pieced in circles, but it is actually nine square blocks set in three rows of three each. Turning the blocks in all directions creates this circular look.

The New York Beauty blocks combine easy foundation piecing and simple curved piecing. You will need to prepare one paper foundation for each block, using the **Arc Pattern** on page 165. For information on paper piecing, see page 248.

You will also need to make templates for pattern pieces A, B, and C on pages 164–165; for information about templates, see page 247. All seam allowances are ¼ inch unless specified otherwise.

CUTTING

Refer to the chart below and cut the required number of strips and pieces. The cut sizes of the rectangular fabric strips include generous seam allowances. With the foundation method, it's easier to work with wider strips. You may wish to decrease the width of the strips by ⅛-inch increments as you become more familiar with this technique. Cut all strips across the crosswise grain, or fabric width. **Note:** Cut and piece one sample block before cutting all the fabric for this quilt.

PIECING THE BLOCKS

Each paper-pieced arc contains background and star point fabrics. Use assorted blue-violets, blues, and violets for the background and assorted yellow-oranges, oranges, and yellows for the star points. The remaining sections of the blocks are cut from templates. See the **Block Diagram.**

Block Diagram

C U T T I N G

FABRIC	Used For	Strip Width (First Cut)	No. to Cut (First Cut)	Shape (Second Cut)	Dimensions (Second Cut)	No. to Cut (Second Cut)
Violet, blue-violet, and blue prints	A	A pieces	7	—	—	—
	C	C pieces	9	—	—	—
	Arc background	—	—	▬	3" × 3½"	45
Dark blue-violet print	Outer border	3¾"	3	—	—	—
Yellow, yellow-orange, and orange prints	A	A pieces	2	—	—	—
	B	B pieces	9	—	—	—
	Star points	—	—	▬	2¼" × 3½"	54
Yellow-orange print	Inner border	1"	2	—	—	—
Binding fabric	Binding	2½"	3	—	—	—

1. Fabric strips are positioned on the back, or unmarked, side of the foundation. Strips are added in numerical order starting at 1. Note that the numbers on this foundation are not in chronological order because of the piecing sequence used. All sewing takes place on the front side of the foundation, directly on the drawn lines. All lines on the foundation, except the dashed one around the outer perimeter, are seam lines. To begin, layer a background strip on top of a star point strip, with right sides together. Position these strips underneath one of the paper piecing foundations, so that the background strip lies against the paper foundation, as shown in **Diagram 1.** The edges of the strips must extend ¼ inch beyond the seam line between 1 and 2 on the paper foundation, as shown. Making 12 to 14 stitches per inch, sew on the line separating 1 and 2, beginning and ending the stitching at the dashed cutting lines, as shown.

Diagram 2

3. Referring to **Diagram 3,** place a background strip right sides together with the 1 and 2 pieces. It may be helpful to pin the loose edge of piece 2 to the foundation to keep it flat while stitching the next strip. Be sure the new background strip extends at least ¼ inch beyond the seam line between 2 and 3, then sew along this seam line.

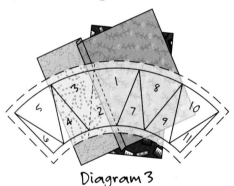

Diagram 3

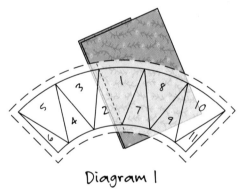

Diagram 1

2. Flip the background strip into a right-side-up position, pressing it firmly in place, as shown in **Diagram 2.** Hold the foundation up to the light with the paper side toward you. You will now be able to see the shadow created by the background fabric. The shadow should overlap all lines drawn for the background piece, and the overlap should be sufficient enough to create a stable seam allowance. If it is not, use a seam ripper to remove the background from the foundation, then reposition the piece and try again. This ensures that there will be sufficient seam allowance on all sides when you add the adjacent fabric strips.

HINTS FROM HAZEL

Use neutral gray thread when sewing blocks containing many colors of fabric. The gray blends nicely with lights or darks and saves time by eliminating the need to change spools when you switch to a new fabric color.

4. Trim fabrics to a scant ¼ inch beyond the seam line between 2 and 3; see **Diagram 4.** Fold the foundation paper away from the fabric to avoid cutting it while you trim the seam allowance.

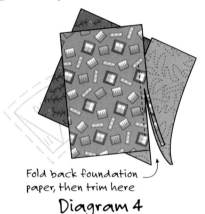

Fold back foundation paper, then trim here

Diagram 4

5. Flip the background piece into a right-side-up position, pressing it firmly in place, as shown in **Diagram 5.**

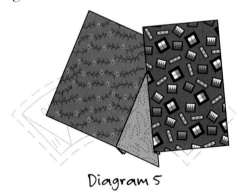

Diagram 5

6. Add the next star point in the same manner as the background piece in Step 3, then trim the seam allowance to a scant ¼ inch. Flip the star point into a right-side-up position and press it firmly in place, as shown in **Diagram 6.**

Diagram 6

7. Continue adding background and star point pieces until the foundation arc is completed. Using scissors, trim the edges of the fabric strips even with the outer dashed line on the foundation paper. Remove the paper foundations.

8. Crease the midpoints of an A piece and a B piece. Make a few clips into the concave (inward) seam allowance of the B piece, so that each clip is approximately ¼ inch apart and about ⅛ inch deep to help ease in any fullness. With the B piece on top, place the right sides of the curved edges together, matching the beginnings, midpoints, and ends of the seam allowances. Pin generously, then sew A and B together, as shown in **Diagram 7.** Press seam toward B.

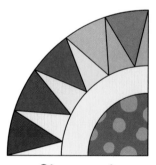

Diagram 7

9. In the same manner, sew the A/B piece to a completed foundation arc; see **Diagram 8.** Clip the inward curve of the pieced arc to ease in any fullness. Press seam toward B.

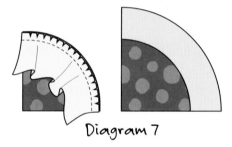

Diagram 8

10. Sew a C piece to the assembled unit to complete the block, as shown in **Diagram 9.** Make ⅛-inch clips in the inward arc of the C piece. Take care to match the endpoints and midpoints, and pin generously before sewing. Press toward C.

Diagram 9

11. Repeat Steps 1 through 10 to make a total of nine blocks. Be sure to use yellow, yellow-orange, or orange for the A piece in two of the blocks.

ASSEMBLING THE QUILT

1. Referring to the **Assembly Diagram,** lay out the completed blocks in three rows of three blocks each. Be sure the blocks are positioned correctly to achieve a circular look.

Assembly Diagram

2. With right sides together, sew the blocks together in three horizontal rows. Press seams in opposite directions from row to row. Sew the rows together. Press seams toward the bottom of the quilt.

Having Fun with Thread

Forget white, black, and tan! The spectrum of quilting thread on the market has grown to include every color of the rainbow. If you're a beginner and your quilting stitches are still a bit uneven, choose a thread color that matches the fabric so the stitches will blend in and be less noticeable. More experienced quilters could use a contrasting thread so the quilting design stands out and becomes as much a part of the quilt as the piecing. Don't be shy about using three or four different colors of quilting thread in the same project.

Metallic quilting threads add a real sparkle to a quilting design, but experiment with them before committing to an entire project. When handquilting, cut a shorter length of thread, since the thread can wear thin as you work. For machine quilting, you may need to use a larger needle and adjust your top tension. These threads come in different weights, strengths, and durabilities and a wide range of colors so you can find one that perfectly suits your quilting needs. New threads are introduced each year, so explore the latest rayons, nylons, silks, Mylars, and wool blends to accent your special quilt.

ADDING THE BORDERS

1. Attach the top and bottom borders first. Measure the width of the quilt top, taking the measurement through the horizontal center of the quilt. Cut two inner border strips this exact length.

2. Fold one of the inner border strips in half crosswise and crease. Unfold it and position it right side down along the top of the quilt, with the crease at the vertical midpoint. Pin at the midpoint and ends first, then along the length of the entire edge, easing in fullness as necessary. Sew the border to the quilt. Repeat for the bottom border. Press seams toward the borders.

3. Measure the length of the quilt, taking the measurement through the vertical center of the quilt and including the top and bottom borders. Cut two inner border strips this exact length.

4. Fold one strip in half crosswise and crease. Unfold it and position it right side down along one side of the quilt, with the crease at the horizontal midpoint. Pin at the midpoint and ends first, then along the length of the entire side, easing in fullness as necessary. Sew the border to the quilt top. Repeat on the opposite side of the quilt. Press seams toward the border.

5. Prepare and add the outer borders to the quilt in the same manner as for the inner borders, sewing on the top and bottom borders first, then the side borders.

QUILTING AND FINISHING

1. Mark the quilt top for quilting. The star points in this quilt were handquilted in the ditch. Continuous curving lines were quilted around the arcs to accentuate the circular-look blocks. Random swirling lines were quilted in the wide outer border.

2. Cut a 28-inch square of backing fabric.

3. Layer the quilt top, batting, and backing, and baste the layers together. Quilt as desired.

4. Make double-fold binding and sew it to the quilt, following the directions on page 250.

Happy Endings ✿ ✦

Continue the outer-space theme by quilting rocket ships, comets, and planets in the border. Sprinkle a few star motifs around the blocks as well. And wouldn't it be fun to make a memory label in the shape of a space shuttle to complete the out-of-this-world look?

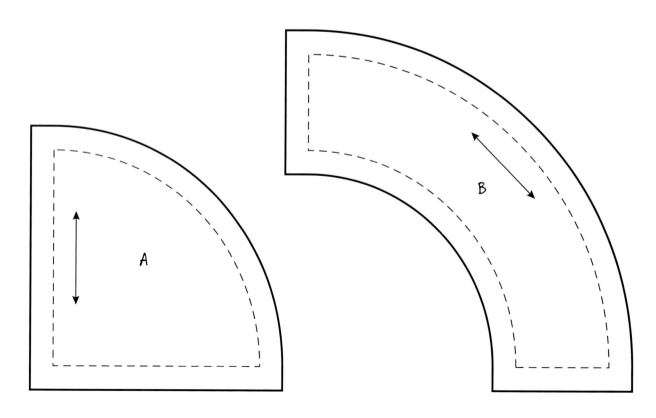

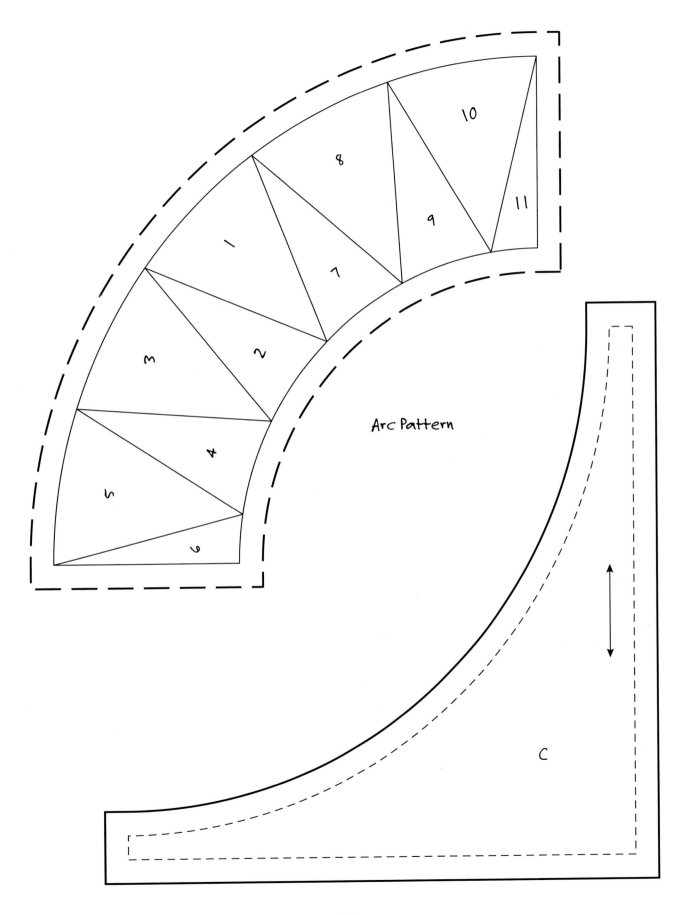

Arc Pattern

C

Windmills and Daisies

A safe starting point when exploring color harmonies, this one-color quilt features all the moods of blue, from a gentle, soothing gray-blue to a very solemn dark blue, with a variety of light, medium, and bright blues added for good measure. Accent this one-color palette with an exciting large-scale print that unifies the many shades and tints used.

Harmony Featured

One Color

Color Used

Blue

MATERIALS

⅝ yard large-scale blue floral print

½ yard very dark blue print

⅜ yard light blue print

⅜ yard dark bright blue print

¼ yard dark blue print

¼ yard medium blue print

¼ yard bright blue print

¼ yard very light blue print

⅞ yard backing fabric

⅜ yard binding fabric

29-inch square of quilt batting

SKILL LEVEL: INTERMEDIATE

Finished Quilt Size: 25" square

Finished Block Size: 4"

Number of Blocks: 9

Magical Beginnings

The blocks in this quilt are paper pieced, so you will need to prepare two paper foundations for each block, using the **Block Pattern** on page 172. For information on preparing foundations and paper piecing, refer to page 248. All seam allowances are ¼ inch unless specified otherwise.

CUTTING

Refer to the chart below and cut the required number of strips, squares, and triangles. Cut all strips across the crosswise grain or fabric width. For this block, you will paper piece with triangles rather than fabric strips because there will be less bulk and less fabric waste. The cut sizes of these triangles include wider-than-necessary seam allowances. The sashing strips and setting pieces are cut larger than necessary. Once the quilt top is assembled, the excess fabric will be trimmed to the appropriate measurement, an easy alternative to time-consuming templates. **Note:** Cut and piece one sample block on a foundation before cutting all the fabric for the quilt.

C U T T I N G

FABRIC	Used For	First Cut — Strip Width	First Cut — No. to Cut	Second Cut — Shape	Second Cut — Dimensions	Second Cut — No. to Cut	Third Cut — Shape	Total No. Needed
Large-scale blue floral print	Setting squares	4½"	1	▢	4½" × 4½"	4	—	—
	Setting triangles	7¼"	1	▢	7¼" × 7¼"	2	⊠	8
	Corner triangles	4¼"	1	▢	4¼" × 4¼"	2	◩	4
Very dark blue print	Sashing	⅞"	3	▬	⅞" × 4½"	18	—	—
	Sashing	⅞"	1	▬	⅞" × 7"	2	—	—
	Sashing	⅞"	1	▬	⅞" × 16"	2	—	—
	Sashing	⅞"	2	▬	⅞" × 25"	2	—	—
	Inner border	1⅛"	4	▬	1⅛" × 29"	4	—	—
Light blue print	Blocks	2¾"	4	▢	2¾" × 2¾"	54	◩	108
Dark bright blue print	Outer border	2"	4	▬	2" × 29"	4	—	—
Dark blue print	Blocks	2¾"	2	▪	2¾" × 2¾"	18	◪	36
Medium blue print	Blocks	2¾"	2	▪	2¾" × 2¾"	18	◪	36
Bright blue print	Middle border	1⅜"	4	▬	1⅜" × 29"	4	—	—
Very light blue print	Blocks	2¼"	2	▢	2¼" × 2¼"	18	�	36
Binding fabric	Binding	2½"	3	—	—	—	—	—

168

PIECING THE BLOCKS

Refer to the **Block Diagram** and **Fabric Key** for fabric placement when paper piecing. Use the dark blue print for triangles 1 and 7, the medium blue print for triangles 4 and 10, the very light blue print for triangles 3 and 9, and the light blue print for triangles 2, 5, 6, 8, 11, and 12.

Block Diagram

FABRIC KEY

Very light blue print   Medium blue print

Light blue print   Dark blue print

1. Fabric triangles are positioned on the back, or unmarked, side of the foundation. Triangles are added in numerical order starting with 1. All sewing takes place on the front side, directly on the drawn lines. All lines on the foundation, except the dashed one around the outer perimeter, are seam lines. To begin, layer triangle 1 on top of triangle 2 with right sides together, as shown in **Diagram 1.** Position these triangles underneath one of the paper piecing foundations, so that triangle 1 lies against the paper foundation, as shown. The edges of the triangles must extend ¼ inch beyond the seam line between 1 and 2 on the paper foundation, as shown. Making 12 to 14 stitches per inch, sew on the line separating 1 and 2, beginning and ending the stitching approximately ¼ inch on either side of the line, as shown.

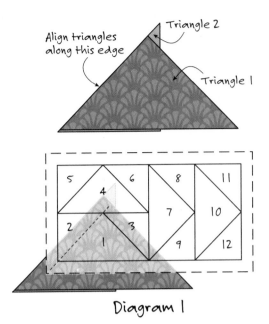

Diagram 1

2. Flip triangle 2 into a right-side-up position, pressing it firmly in place; see **Diagram 2.** Then hold the foundation up to the light with the paper side toward you. You will now be able to see the shadow created by triangle 2. The shadow should overlap all lines drawn for triangle 2, and the overlap should be sufficient to create a stable seam allowance. If it is not, use a seam ripper to remove the background from the foundation, then reposition the piece and try again.

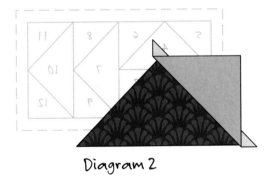

Diagram 2

3. Referring to **Diagram 3,** place triangle 3 right sides together with triangles 1 and 2. It may be helpful to pin triangle 2 to the foundation to keep it smooth while adding triangle 3. Flip the foundation over so the paper side is facing you. Be sure triangle 3 extends at least ¼ inch beyond the seam line between 1 and 3, then sew along this seam line.

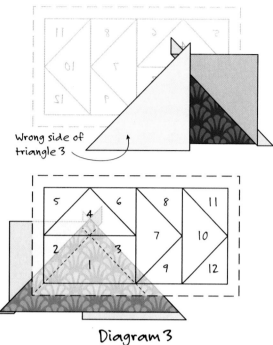

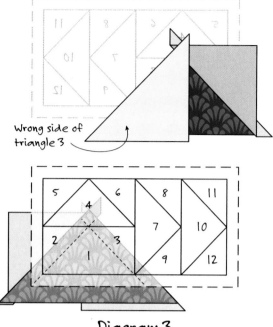

Diagram 3

4. Trim triangles 1 and 3 to a scant ¼-inch seam allowance; see **Diagram 4.** Fold back the foundation paper to avoid cutting it. Flip triangle 3 into a right-side-up position and press it in place.

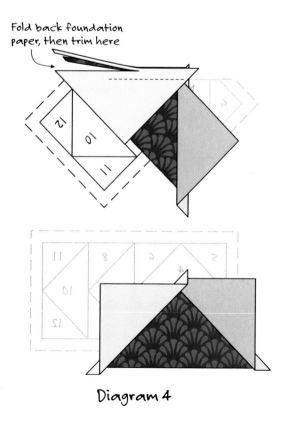

Diagram 4

5. Align and sew triangle 4 so at least ¼ inch of the long edge extends beyond the seam line between 4 and 2/1/3; see **Diagram 5.** Trim the seam allowance. Press in place.

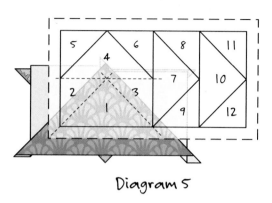

Diagram 5

6. Referring to Steps 3 and 4, add triangles 5 and 6, and trim the seam allowance in the same manner as for triangle 3.

7. Referring to **Diagram 6,** align and sew triangle 7 so at least ¼ inch of the long edge extends beyond the seam line between 7 and 6/4/3/1. Trim the seam allowance, then flip and press triangle 7.

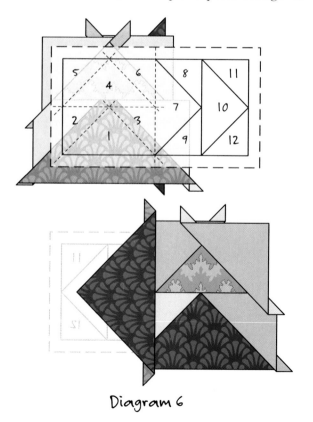

Diagram 6

8. Add the remaining triangles to the foundation, trimming seam allowances as you work.

9. Repeat Steps 1 through 8 to make the second half of the block. Use a rotary cutter and ruler to trim the block on the outer dashed lines. Remove the paper foundations. With right sides of the fabric together, pin and sew the two halves of the block together, matching the center points.

10. Repeat Steps 1 through 9 to make a total of nine blocks.

ASSEMBLING THE QUILT

1. Use a design wall or other flat surface to lay out the pieced blocks, setting squares and triangles, corner triangles, and sashing strips, referring to the **Assembly Diagram.**

Assembly Diagram

2. Sew all pieces into diagonal rows, as shown. Press the seams toward the sashing strips. Sew the rows together, matching seams carefully. Use your rotary cutter and ruler to trim the oversize sashing strips and setting and corner triangles to within ½ inch of the corner of the pieced blocks to create a straight edge, as shown in **Diagram 7.**

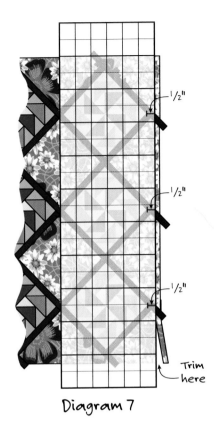

½"

½"

½"

Trim here

Diagram 7

ADDING THE BORDERS

1. Sew the inner border to the middle and outer borders. Treat the borders as one unit. Press the seams toward the outer border. Repeat to make four borders.

2. Read "Mitered Borders" on pages 248–249. Make the 45 degree angle cuts and mark the ¼-inch seam intersections as directed. Repeat for all four borders. Find the center of each border by folding it in half and marking the midpoint with a pin. Find the center of each quilt side by folding and marking with a pin. With right sides together, pin each border to the quilt, beginning at the center. Pin at each ¼-inch seam intersection, then generously pin the remaining areas, easing in any fullness. Sew each border to the quilt, stopping and starting at the marked ¼-inch seam intersections.

3. Miter the corner seams, referring to page 249 for details.

QUILTING AND FINISHING

1. Mark quilting designs as desired. The blocks and borders in this quilt were handquilted in the ditch. A daisy was quilted in the setting squares, and a half daisy was quilted in the setting triangles.

2. Cut a 29-inch square of backing fabric.

3. Layer the quilt top, batting, and backing, and baste the layers together. Quilt as desired.

4. Make double-fold binding and sew it to the quilt, following the directions on page 250.

Happy Endings

Wallhangings can accumulate dust quickly. Take your quilt outside every month and gently shake it. Or toss the quilt in the dryer and give it a few tumbles. A little care will go a long way toward keeping your handiwork bright and soil-free.

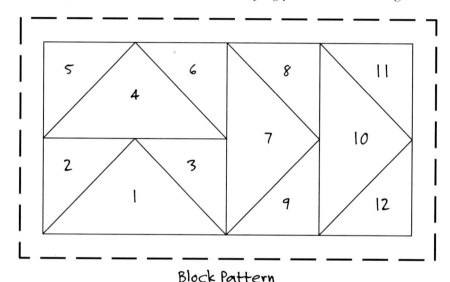

Block Pattern

Lap-Size Quilt

Finished Quilt Size: 53¼" square   **Finished Block Size: 8"**   **Number of Blocks: 9**

MATERIALS

1 yard large-scale blue floral print
¾ yard very dark blue print
1⅛ yards light blue print
1 yard dark bright blue print
⅝ yard dark blue print
⅝ yard medium blue print

⅜ yard bright blue print
½ yard very light blue print
3⅛ yards backing fabric
½ yard binding fabric
53-inch square of quilt batting

DIRECTIONS

1. Read the Windmills and Daisies project for color and fabric information, basic directions, and helpful tips.

2. Follow the directions in "Piecing the Blocks" on pages 169–171 to make nine pieced blocks; use the **Lap-Size Block Pattern** on page 174 for the foundation.

3. Follow the directions in "Assembling the Quilt" and "Adding the Borders" on page 171, piecing the sashing and border strips as necessary, to assemble the quilt top. Press the block seams toward the sashing strips.

4. For the backing, cut the backing fabric in half crosswise. Cut 27-inch-wide segments from each of the pieces. Sew the segments together along the long edge, as shown in the **Backing Diagram.** Press the seams open.

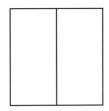

Backing Diagram

5. Layer the quilt top, batting, and backing and baste the layers together. Quilt as desired. Make double-fold binding and sew it to the quilt top, following the directions on page 250.

C U T T I N G

| FABRIC | Used For | First Cut | | Second Cut | | | Third Cut | |
		Strip Width	No. to Cut	Shape	Dimensions	No. to Cut	Shape	Total No. Needed
Large-scale blue floral print	Setting triangles	12¾"	1	▪	12¾" × 12¾"	2	◩	8
	Setting squares	8½"	1	▪	8½" × 8½"	4	—	—
	Corner triangles	8½"	1	▪	8½" × 8½"	2	◸	4
Very dark blue print	Sashing	1⅛"	5	▬	1⅛" × 8½"	18	—	—
	Sashing	1⅛"	1	▬	1⅛" × 12"	2	—	—
	Sashing	1⅛"	2	▬	1⅛" × 34"	2	—	—
	Sashing	1⅛"	3*	▬	1⅛" × 50"	2	—	—
	Inner border	1¼"	6†	▬	1¼" × 54"	4	—	—
Light blue print	Blocks	3¾"	7	▪	3¾" × 3¾"	54	◸	108
Dark bright blue print	Outer border	5"	6†	▬	5" × 54"	4	—	—
Dark blue print	Blocks	4½"	3	▪	4½" × 4½"	18	◸	36
Medium blue print	Blocks	4½"	3	▪	4½" × 4½"	18	◸	36
Bright blue print	Middle border	1¾"	6†	▬	1¾" × 54"	4	—	—
Very light blue print	Blocks	4½"	3	▫	4½" × 4½"	18	◸	36
Binding fabric	Binding	2¼"	6	—	—	—	—	—

*Piece these three strips together, then cut into 50-inch lengths.

†Piece these six strips together, then cut into 54-inch lengths.

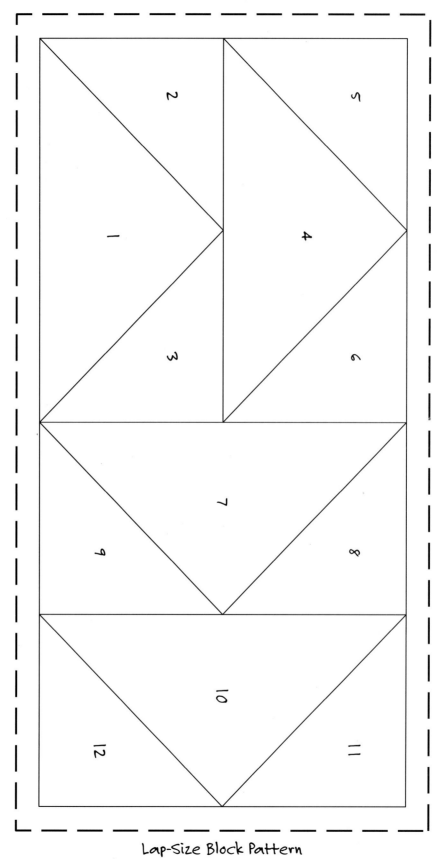

Lap-Size Block Pattern

Seascape

Echoing the colors of the deep, this water-inspired quilt shown on page 176 features the Three Side-by-Side Colors harmony of blue, blue-green, and green. These neighboring colors flow naturally along the color wheel, creating a palette that includes almost a dozen fabrics.

shown on page 176

Harmony Featured

Three Side-by-Side Colors

Colors Used

Blue, blue-green, green

MATERIALS

¼ yard light blue print for center medallion

½ yard dark blue marbleized print

½ yard light blue marbleized print

⅜ yard medium blue floral print

½ yard dark blue-green floral print

⅜ yard blue-green swirled print

⅜ yard blue-green mottled print

¼ yard blue-green floral print

⅝ yard green swirled print

⅜ yard light green marbleized print

1 yard neutral marbleized print

1 yard backing fabric

⅜ yard binding fabric

30-inch square of quilt batting

Assorted bugle and seed beads and pearls

SKILL LEVEL: ADVANCED

Finished Quilt Size: 27½" square

Finished Quilt Center Size: 18" square

Finished Border Block Size: 4½" × 4¾"

Magical Beginnings

"Special effects" fabrics can bring an exciting dimension to your quilt. Fabric texture, or the illusion of it, creates a feast for the eyes. While the actual fabrics in the quilt are flat and untextured, the marbleized and swirling prints mimic the wave action of the sea. Buy, trade, or collect watery-look blue, blue-green, and green fabrics to provide the drama for this design. The sea anemone in the center of the quilt was pieced from a carefully cut floral fabric; try to find a similar print to achieve the same effect.

C U T T I N G

| | | First Cut | | Second Cut | | | Third Cut | |
FABRIC	Used For	Strip Width	No. to Cut	Shape	Dimensions	No. to Cut	Shape	Total No. Needed
Light blue print	D	D pieces	8	—	—	—	—	—
Dark blue marbleized print	B and B reverse and C and C reverse	4½"	3	—	—	—	—	—
Light blue marbleized print	B and B reverse	3¾"	2	—	—	—	—	—
	C and C reverse	4"	1	—	—	—	—	—
Medium blue floral print	A and A reverse	5½"	2	—	—	—	—	—
Dark blue-green floral print	B and B reverse and C and C reverse	6"	2	—	—	—	—	—
Blue-green swirled print	A and A reverse	4¾"	2	—	—	—	—	—
Blue-green mottled print	A and A reverse	5½"	1	—	—	—	—	—
Blue-green floral print	B and B reverse	3½"	2	—	—	—	—	—
Green swirled print	B and B reverse	6¼"	2	—	—	—	—	—
	C and C reverse	3¼"	1	—	—	—	—	—
Light green marbleized print	A and A reverse	4¾"	2	—	—	—	—	—
Neutral marbleized print	A and A reverse	5½"	2	—	—	—	—	—
	B and B reverse	6¼"	2	—	—	—	—	—
	C and C reverse	2¾"	1	—	—	—	—	—
	Triangles	6¼"	1	▢	6¼" × 6¼"	2	◪	4
Binding fabric	Binding	2½"	3	—	—	—	—	—

This design uses a combination of quilt-making techniques—paper piecing, rotary cutting, and templates. For the paper-pieced sections, prepare the paper foundations for A, A reverse, B, B reverse, C, and C reverse on pages 184 to 185. For information on preparing foundations and paper piecing, refer to page 248.

To make a reverse foundation, trace or photocopy the pattern in the usual manner. Then turn the paper over so the lines are on the bottom side, and use a light box to trace the lines that show through onto the blank side of the paper. Label the newly marked side "sewing side" and the side with the original lines "fabric side." You will also need to make a template for pattern piece D on page 185; for information about making and using templates, see page 247. All seam allowances are ¼ inch unless otherwise indicated.

CUTTING

Refer to the cutting chart on page 177 and cut the required number of strips and pieces. The cut sizes of the fabric strips include generous seam allowances. With the foundation method, it's easier to work with wider strips, especially when you are paper piecing odd shapes. However, since it will only take a practice block or two for you to become comfortable with foundation piecing, you may not want to cut extra-wide strips for the entire quilt. You may wish to decrease the width of the strips by ⅛-inch increments as you become more familiar with this technique. Never cut strips narrower than the finished width plus ¼-inch seam allowance on each side. Cut all strips across the crosswise grain, or fabric width. **Note:** Cut and piece one sample of each unit on a foundation before cutting all the fabric for this quilt.

Work a Little Color Magic

Planning a Center Medallion

If you plan a medallion-look motif like the sea anemone in the center of this quilt, try using two mirrors to audition suitable fabrics. First, cut a clear plastic template for piece D, omitting the seam allowances. Tape two mirrors together along one edge so they can be opened to any angle. Butt the open mirrors to the edges of D (at the small point) to create a 45 degree angle.

Carefully tape the open mirrors together across the top to secure the angle.

Lay your print fabric flat and place the angled mirrors on it. Move the mirrors around on the fabric to find a suitable design. If you find a spot that's pleasing, nestle template D into the hinge of the mirrors to see the amount of the print that will show. The eight mirror reflections will give you a reasonably accurate idea of how your medallion motif will look after it's pieced. To guarantee that you'll cut at exactly the same spot across the fabric repeats, use a permanent ink marker to draw the fabric motif outline directly on the template. Each time you use the template, place it on the fabric in the same position, using the permanent ink markings as a placement guide.

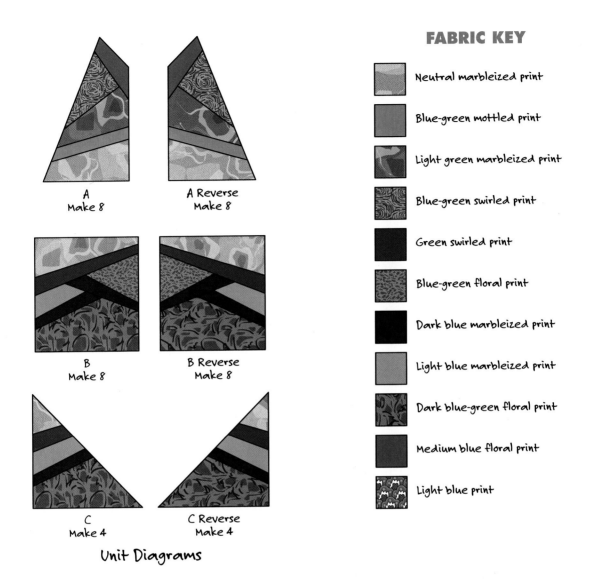

FABRIC KEY

Neutral marbleized print

Blue-green mottled print

Light green marbleized print

Blue-green swirled print

Green swirled print

Blue-green floral print

Dark blue marbleized print

Light blue marbleized print

Dark blue-green floral print

Medium blue floral print

Light blue print

A
Make 8

A Reverse
Make 8

B
Make 8

B Reverse
Make 8

C
Make 4

C Reverse
Make 4

Unit Diagrams

PIECING THE BLOCKS

These instructions direct you in piecing one of the three foundation units used for this quilt. While the shapes and color placements are different for each block, the process is the same. Be sure to label your fabrics to avoid confusion. As you piece each unit, refer to the **Unit Diagrams** and **Fabric Key** for fabric placement.

1. Fabric pieces are positioned on the back, or unmarked, side of the paper foundation. Pieces are added in numerical order starting at 1; to avoid lengthy color names in these instructions, fabrics will be referred to by their position number on the foundation. All sewing takes place on the front side of the foundation, directly on the drawn lines. All lines on the foundation, except the dashed one around the outer perimeter, are seam lines. To begin, layer piece 2 on top of piece 1 with right sides together. Position these pieces underneath one of the paper-piecing foundations, so that the wrong side of piece 1 lies against the paper foundation, as shown in **Diagram 1** on page 180. The edges of the piece must extend ¼ inch beyond the seam line between 1 and 2 on the foundation, as shown in the diagram. Using 12 to 14 stitches per inch, sew on the line separating 1 and 2, beginning and ending the stitching approximately ¼ inch on either side of the line, as shown.

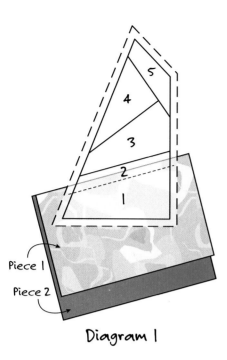

Diagram 1

3. Referring to **Diagram 3,** place piece 3 right sides together with pieces 1 and 2. Be sure piece 3 extends at least ¼ inch beyond the seam line between 2 and 3, then sew along this seam line.

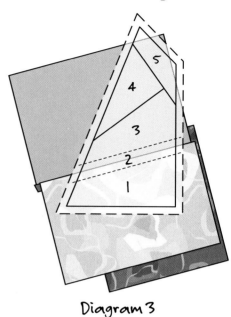

Diagram 3

2. Flip piece 2 into a right-side-up position, pressing it in place; see **Diagram 2.** Hold the foundation up to the light with the paper side toward you. You will now be able to see the shadow created by piece 2. The shadow should overlap all lines drawn for piece 2. If it does not, use a seam ripper to remove piece 2 from the foundation, then reposition it and try again. This ensures that there will be enough seam allowance on all sides when you add the adjacent fabric pieces.

4. Trim pieces 2 and 3 to a scant ¼ inch beyond the seam line; see **Diagram 4.** Fold the foundation away from the fabric to avoid cutting it while you trim the seam allowance. Flip piece 3 into a right-side-up position, pressing it in place.

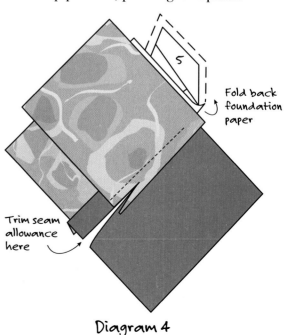

Diagram 4

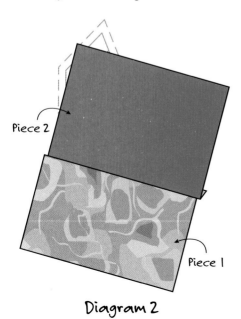

Diagram 2

5. Add piece 4 in the same manner as piece 3 was added in Step 4; see **Diagram 5.**

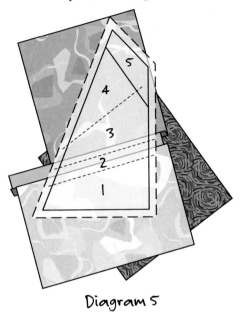

Diagram 5

6. Add piece 5 in the same manner as piece 4 was added; see **Diagram 6.** Trim the edges of the block on the outer dashed lines. Do not remove the paper foundations yet.

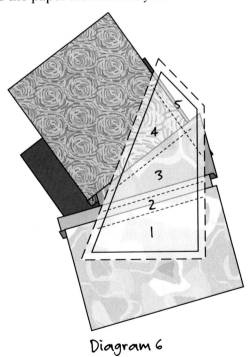

Diagram 6

7. Repeat Steps 1 through 5 to make A reverse, using the appropriate foundation.

8. Using the **Unit Diagrams** and the **Fabric Key** on page 179, paper piece foundations B, B reverse, C, and C reverse. Trim the edges of the block on the outer dashed lines.

ASSEMBLING THE QUILT CENTER

1. To make a center medallion point, place the right sides of A and A reverse together, then sew from the lower edge, ending at the dot. Backstitch at the dot, as shown in **Diagram 7.** Do not press.

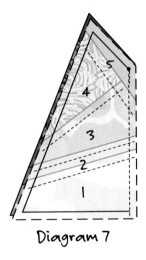

Diagram 7

2. Repeat Step 1 to make a total of eight A/A reverse units. Do not press.

3. Pin D and the A reverse section of the A/A reverse unit with right sides together, matching the small sides. Sew from the dot to the outer edge; see **Diagram 8.** Do not press.

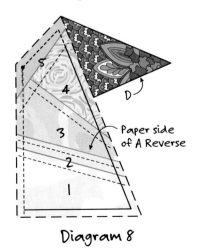

Paper side of A Reverse

Diagram 8

4. Repeat Step 3 to sew the remaining short side of D to the A section, as shown in **Diagram 9.** Press the center seam of A/A reverse toward A and the two D seams toward A and A reverse.

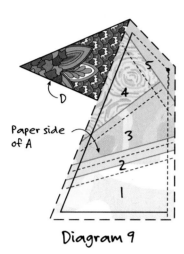

Diagram 9

5. Repeat Steps 1 through 4 to make a total of eight center medallion points.

6. With right sides together and seams matched carefully, sew four center medallion points together, forming one-half of the center pattern; see **Diagram 10.** Press seams toward A reverse. Repeat for the remaining half of the center pattern. Remove the paper foundations, taking care not to stretch the fabric or seam lines.

Diagram 10

7. With right sides together, sew the two center pattern halves together to form a hexagon. Press the seam to one side. Handle the hexagon carefully at this point to avoid stretching it.

8. With right sides together, center and sew a neutral marbleized print triangle to one corner of the hexagon, as shown in **Diagram 11.** Press the seam toward the triangle. Sew the remaining triangles to the three other corners of the hexagon to form a square. The corner triangles were cut slightly larger than necessary to avoid odd rotary-cutting measurements. After sewing, trim the triangle edges even with the quilt edge.

Diagram 11

HINTS FROM HAZEL

To perfectly align the corner triangle, fold it in half along the bias edge and finger crease the midpoint, taking care not to stretch this edge. Align the crease of the triangle with the seamline of A/A reverse and pin. The triangle is aligned correctly if the tips of the triangle extend beyond the edges of the hexagon.

ASSEMBLING THE BORDER BLOCKS

1. To make a border block, place the right sides of B and B reverse together and sew, taking care to match seams on the foundations. Press the seam toward B.

2. Repeat Step 1 to make a total of eight B/B reverse units.

3. With right sides together, sew two B/B reverse units together to form a four-block border unit, matching seams on the foundations. Press the seam toward B reverse.

4. Repeat Step 3 to make a total of four 4-block border units.

5. To make a corner block, place the right sides of C and C reverse together and sew the long diagonal side, taking care to match seams on the foundations. Press the seam toward C.

6. Repeat Step 5 to make a total of four C/C reverse units. Remove all paper foundations, handling the blocks carefully to avoid stretching them.

ASSEMBLING THE QUILT

1. With right sides together and the neutral marbleized prints aligned, sew a four-block border unit to the top and bottom of the quilt, carefully matching seams on the foundations. Press seams toward the border.

2. With right sides together and seams matched, sew a corner block to each end of the remaining two border units to form side borders; be sure the neutral marbleized prints are aligned. Press seams toward the border unit.

3. With right sides together, sew a side border to each side of the quilt, matching seams on the foundations; be sure the neutral marbleized prints are aligned. See **Diagram 12.** Press seams toward the border.

Diagram 12

QUILTING AND FINISHING

1. Mark quilting designs as desired. The center of this quilt was handquilted in the ditch. In the areas with larger fabric pieces, flowing lines were handquilted to continue the ocean water theme. The smaller fabric pieces were accented with in-the-ditch quilting stitches.

2. Cut a 30-inch square of backing fabric.

3. Layer the quilt top, batting, and backing, and baste the layers together. Quilt as desired.

4. Make double-fold binding and sew it to the quilt, following the directions on page 250.

Happy Endings

Add a bit of ocean whimsy to the Seascape quilt by adding "buried treasure" in the form of beads and pearls. Select subtly colored metallic beads and sew them onto seam lines and at seam intersections to keep them as unobtrusive as a pirate's riches. Add iridescent pearls around the center medallion to continue the jewels-of-the-deep theme.

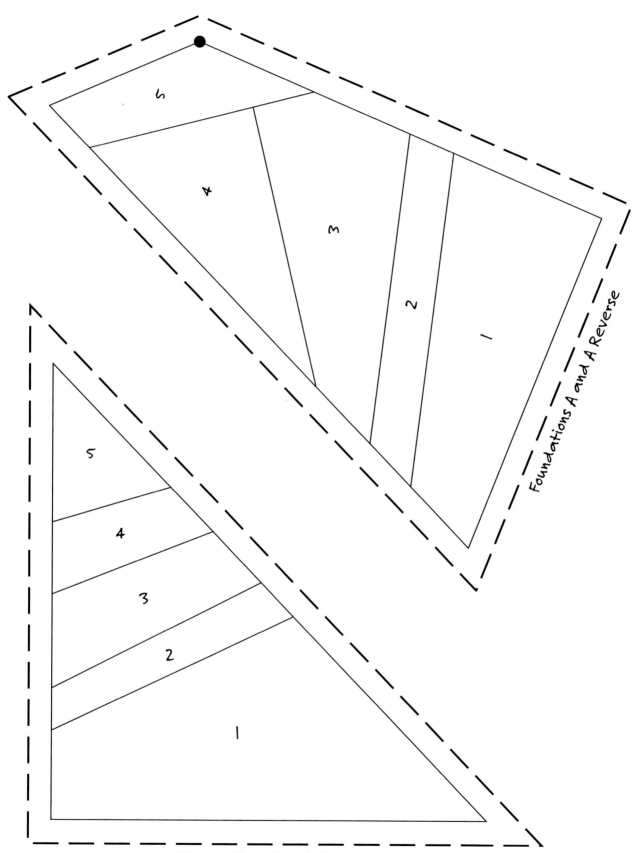

Foundations A and A Reverse

Foundations C and C Reverse

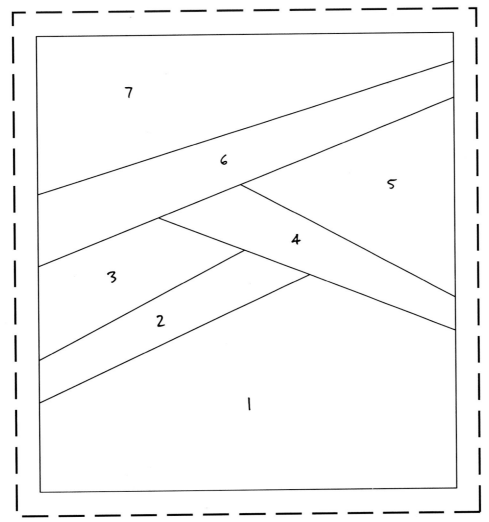

Foundations B and B Reverse

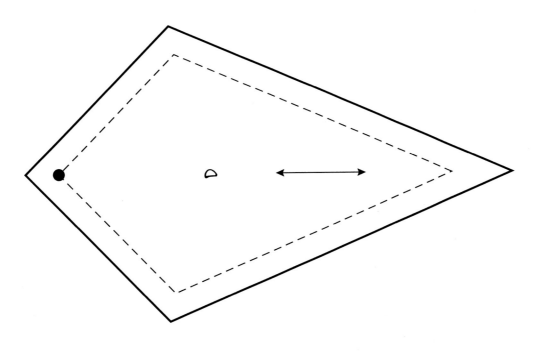

Sailboats

When color wheel colors are tinted to pastels, the effect is soft, comforting, and very cute. Using the harmony Three Alternating Colors with an Accent, this quilt combines three colors on one side of the color wheel, then adds a zinger from the opposite side to create a palette with snap! The "islands" of green and "waves" of blue bring a touch of symbolic whimsy.

Harmony Featured

Three Alternating Colors with an Accent

Colors Used

Green, blue, violet, accent of orange

MATERIALS

⅜ yard total of assorted green prints

⅛ yard light blue print

⅛ yard medium blue print

¼ yard dark blue print

¼ yard total of assorted violet prints

¼ yard total of assorted orange prints

½ yard multicolor print

1 yard white print

⅞ yard backing fabric

⅜ yard binding fabric

29-inch square of quilt batting

SKILL LEVEL: EASY

Finished Quilt Size: 25" square

Finished Block Size: 5"

Number of Sailboat Blocks: 5

Number of Checkerboard Blocks: 4

Magical Beginnings

This quilt uses rotary cutting and paper piecing techniques. The Sailboat blocks are paper pieced, so you will need to prepare one paper foundation for each block, using the **Sailboat Block Pattern** on page 193. For information on preparing foundations and paper piecing, refer to page 248.

The Sailboat and Checkerboard blocks in this quilt contain an assortment of prints in green, violet, and orange. To create a scrappy look, purchase a ⅛-yard cut of a variety of fabrics, or make the blocks out of the same print for a uniform appearance. All seam allowances are ¼ inch unless specified otherwise.

C U T T I N G

FABRIC	Used For	First Cut Strip Width	First Cut No. to Cut	Second Cut Shape	Second Cut Dimensions	Second Cut No. to Cut	Third Cut Shape	Third Cut Total No. Needed
Assorted green prints	Checkerboard blocks	1½"	3	▬	1½" × 18"	5	—	—
	Inner border	1½"	1	—	—	—	—	—
Light blue print	Inner border	1½"	1	—	—	—	—	—
Medium blue print	Inner border	1½"	1	—	—	—	—	—
Dark blue print	Middle border	1"	4	—	—	—	—	—
Assorted violet prints	Sailboat blocks	2½"	1	▬	2½" × 6½"	5	—	—
Assorted orange prints	Sailboat blocks	3¾"	1	▬	3¾" × 5¼"	5	—	—
Multicolor print	Outer border	3"	4	—	—	—	—	—
White print	Checkerboard blocks	1½"	2	▭	1½" × 18"	3	—	—
	Checkerboard blocks	2½"	1	▭	2½" × 18"	2	—	—
	Checkerboard blocks	3½"	1	▭	3½" × 18"	1	—	—
	Sailboat blocks	4½"	1	▭	4½" × 7"	5	—	—
	Sailboat blocks	2¼"	1	▭	2¼" × 5¼"	5	—	—
	Sailboat blocks	3½"	1	▢	3½" × 3½"	5	◺	10
	Inner border	2½"	1	▭	2½" × 4½"	8	—	—
	Inner border	1½"	3	—	—	—	—	—
Binding fabric	Binding	2½"	3	—	—	—	—	—

CUTTING

Refer to the chart on the opposite page and cut the required number of strips and pieces. The cut sizes of the fabric strips for the paper-pieced Sailboat blocks include generous seam allowances. You may wish to decrease the width of the strips by ⅛-inch increments as you become more familiar with this technique. Cut all strips across the crosswise grain, or fabric width. **Note:** Cut and piece one sample Checkerboard block and one sample Sailboat block on a foundation before cutting all the fabric for the quilt.

PIECING THE CHECKERBOARD BLOCKS

The strip sets used for the Checkerboard block are shown in the **Strip Set Diagrams.** Gray is used in the diagrams to represent the white print fabric.

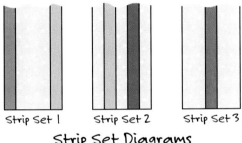

Strip Set 1   Strip Set 2   Strip Set 3

Strip Set Diagrams

1. To make Strip Set 1, sew one 1½-inch green strip to each side of a 3½-inch white strip. Press the seams in the same direction. Square up one end of the set, then cut eight 1½-inch segments from it; see **Diagram 1.**

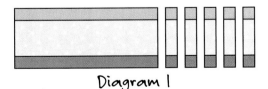

Diagram 1

2. To make Strip Set 2, sew 1½-inch strips together lengthwise in the following order: white, green, white, green, and white. Press all seams in the same direction. Square up one end, then cut eight 1½-inch segments from it; see **Diagram 2.**

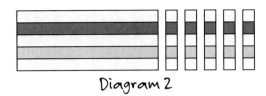

Diagram 2

3. To make Strip Set 3, sew one 2½-inch white strip to each side of a 1½-inch green segment. Press all seams in the same direction. Square up one end of the set, then cut four 1½-inch segments from it; see **Diagram 3.**

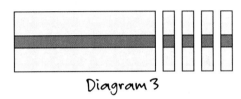

Diagram 3

4. To assemble the Checkerboard block, position two Strip Set 1 segments, two Strip Set 2 segments, and one Strip Set 3 segment, as shown in **Diagram 4,** with the seams facing in opposite directions. Sew the segments in each block together. Press the seams away from the center segment.

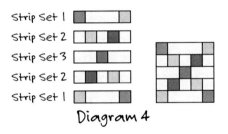

Strip Set 1
Strip Set 2
Strip Set 3
Strip Set 2
Strip Set 1

Diagram 4

5. Repeat Steps 1 through 4 to make a total of four Checkerboard blocks.

PIECING THE SAILBOAT BLOCKS

1. Fabric strips are positioned on the back, or unmarked, side of the foundation. Strips are added in numerical order starting at 1. All sewing takes place on the front side, directly on the drawn lines. All lines on the foundation, except the dashed one around the outer perimeter, are seam lines. To begin, layer piece 1 (orange sail) on top of piece 2 (2¼ × 5¼-inch white sky) with right sides together.

Position these strips underneath a foundation, so that piece 1 lies against the foundation; see **Diagram 5.** The edges of the strips must extend ¼ inch beyond the seam line between 1 and 2. Making 12 to 14 stitches per inch, sew on the line separating 1 and 2, beginning and ending the stitching ¼ inch on either side of the line.

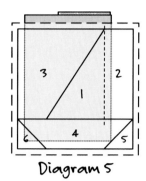

Diagram 5

2. Flip piece 2 into a right-side-up position, pressing it in place; see **Diagram 6.** Hold the foundation up to the light with the paper side toward you. You will now be able to see the shadow created by piece 2. The shadow should overlap all lines drawn for piece 2. If it does not, remove the pieces from the foundation, then reposition them and try again. This ensures that there will be enough seam allowance on all sides when you add the adjacent fabric strips.

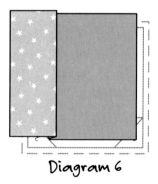

Diagram 6

3. Referring to **Diagram 7,** place piece 3 (4½ × 7-inch white sky) right sides together with the 1 and 2 pieces. Pin the loose edges of pieces 1 and 2 to the foundation to avoid lumps when adding the next strip. Be sure piece 3 extends at least ¼ inch beyond the seam line between 1 and 3, then sew along this seam line.

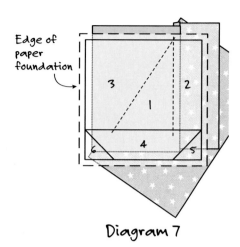

Diagram 7

4. Trim pieces 1 and 3 to a scant ¼ inch beyond the seam line between 1 and 3; see **Diagram 8.** Fold the foundation away from the fabric to avoid cutting it while you trim the seam allowance. Flip piece 3 into a right-side-up position. Trim piece 3 about ¼ inch beyond the outer dashed lines.

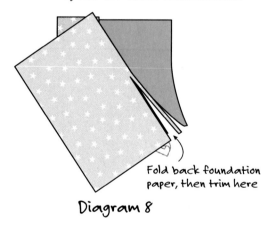

Fold back foundation paper, then trim here

Diagram 8

5. Position piece 4 (violet boat) right sides together with the 1, 2, and 3 pieces. Be sure piece 4 extends at least ¼ inch below the 3/1/2 and 4 seam line, then sew this seam; see **Diagram 9.**

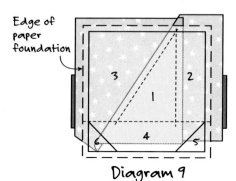

Diagram 9

6. To finish the corners, place piece 5 (3½-inch white sky triangle) right sides together with pieces 2 and 4, and sew the seam line between 4 and 5; see **Diagram 10.** Trim the seam, then flip and press the piece into a right-side-up position. Add the remaining corner in the same manner.

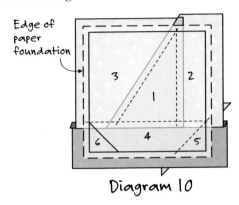

Diagram 10

7. Use a rotary cutter and ruler to trim the block's edges on the outer dashed lines; see **Diagram 11.**

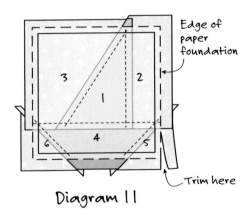

Diagram 11

8. Repeat Steps 1 through 7 to make a total of five Sailboat blocks. Remove the paper foundations.

ASSEMBLING THE QUILT

1. Referring to the photograph, lay out the completed blocks in three rows of three blocks each, alternating the Sailboat and Checkerboard blocks.

2. With right sides together, sew the blocks together in horizontal rows. Press seams in opposite directions from row to row.

3. With right sides together, sew the rows of blocks together, matching seams carefully. Press the seam allowances toward the bottom edge of the quilt.

PIECING THE INNER BORDER

1. With right sides together, sew one 1½-inch white strip to a 1½-inch green strip. Press the seam toward the green. Square up one end of the strip set, then cut twelve 1½-inch segments from it; see **Diagram 12.**

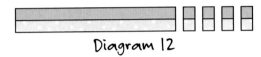

Diagram 12

2. To assemble the green Checkerboard unit for the inner border, position three green-and-white segments as shown in **Diagram 13.** Sew the segments together, matching seam intersections carefully. Press the seam to one side.

Diagram 13

3. Repeat Steps 1 and 2 to make four green-and-white Checkerboard units.

4. With right sides together, sew one 1½-inch white strip to a 1½-inch light blue strip. Press the seam toward the light blue. Square up one end of the strip set, then cut sixteen 1½-inch segments from it; see **Diagram 14.**

Diagram 14

5. To assemble the light blue Checkerboard unit for the inner border, position two light blue–and–white segments as shown in **Diagram 15.** Sew the segments together, matching seam intersections carefully. Press the seam to one side.

Diagram 15

6. Repeat Steps 4 and 5 to make a total of eight light blue–and-white Checkerboard units.

7. Repeat Steps 4 and 5 to make four medium blue–and-white Checkerboard units.

8. Referring to **Diagram 16,** position and sew two light blue–and-white Checkerboard units, two 2½ × 4½-inch white rectangles, and one green-and-white Checkerboard unit, as shown, to create the inner border. Be sure the green and blue squares in the Checkerboard units are positioned properly. Repeat to make four inner borders.

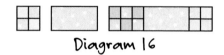

Diagram 16

9. Fold one of the inner borders in half crosswise and crease it. Unfold it and position it right side down along the top of the quilt, with the crease at the vertical midpoint. Pin at the midpoint and ends first, then along the length of the entire edge, matching seams and easing in fullness as necessary. Sew the border to the quilt. Repeat for the bottom inner border. Press the seams toward the border.

10. Sew one medium blue Checkerboard unit to each end of the two remaining inner borders, as shown in **Diagram 17.**

Diagram 17

11. With right sides together, sew the side inner borders to the quilt in the same manner as the top and bottom inner borders, being sure the Checkerboard units are positioned properly. See the **Quilt Diagram.**

Quilt Diagram

ADDING THE MIDDLE AND OUTER BORDERS

1. Attach the top and bottom middle border first. Measure the width of the quilt top, taking the measurement through the horizontal center of the quilt. Cut two middle border strips this length.

2. Fold one of the middle border strips in half crosswise and crease. Unfold it and position it right side down along the top of the quilt, with the crease at the vertical midpoint. Pin at the midpoint and ends first, then along the length of the entire edge. Sew the border to the quilt. Repeat for the bottom border. Press seams toward the border.

3. Measure the length of the quilt, taking the measurement through the vertical center of the quilt and including the top and bottom borders. Cut two middle border strips this exact length.

4. Fold one strip in half crosswise and crease. Unfold it and position it right side down along one side of the quilt, with the crease at the horizontal midpoint. Pin at the midpoint and ends first, then along the length of the entire side. Sew the border to the quilt top. Repeat on the opposite side of the quilt. Press seams toward the border.

5. Prepare and add the outer borders in the same manner as for the inner borders, sewing on the top and bottom borders first.

QUILTING AND FINISHING

1. Mark quilting designs as desired. The Checkerboard blocks were handquilted in the ditch, the hulls with lines, the sails with squares, and the skies with diagonal sunbeams.

2. Cut a 29-inch square of backing fabric.

3. Layer the quilt top, batting, and backing, and baste the layers together. Quilt as desired.

4. Make double-fold binding and sew it to the quilt, following the directions on page 250.

Happy Endings

Create a memory book to record details about your projects! Use a separate page for each quilt, listing the yardage you needed. Add a swatch of each fabric, a photo of the quilt, and pattern number or directions source. Include any thoughts about your inspiration, the quilt's recipient, and the date of completion. In years to come, you can look back through the pages of your memory book and recall the joy of creating each special quilt.

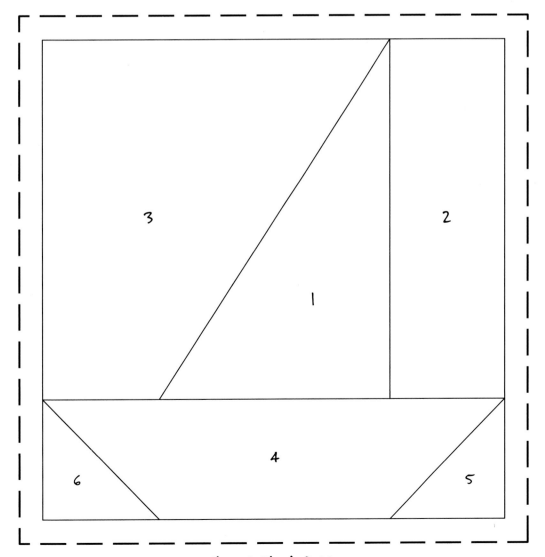

Sailboat Block Pattern

Large Wallhanging

Finished Quilt Size: 65¾" square **Finished Block Size: 8¾"**
Number of Sailboat Blocks: 13 **Number of Checkerboard Blocks: 12**

MATERIALS

1 yard total of assorted green prints

⅛ yard light blue print

⅛ yard medium blue print

½ yard dark blue print

⅝ yard total of assorted violet prints

⅝ yard total of assorted orange prints

1⅜ yard multicolor print

3⅞ yards white print

4 yards backing fabric

⅝ yard binding fabric

70-inch square of quilt batting

DIRECTIONS

1. Read the Sailboats project for color and fabric information, basic directions, and helpful tips.

2. Follow the directions in "Piecing the Checkerboard Blocks" and "Piecing the Sailboat Blocks" on page 189 to make 13 Sailboat blocks and 12 Checkerboard blocks; use the **Large Wallhanging Block Pattern** for the Sailboat blocks.

3. Referring to the **Large Wallhanging Diagram,** lay out the blocks in five rows of five blocks each, alternating the blocks. Follow the directions in "Assembling the Quilt" on page 191 to sew the blocks and rows together.

4. To piece the inner borders, follow the directions in "Piecing the Inner Border" on page 191, using two green-and-white Checkerboard units, two light blue–and–white Checkerboard units, two 4 × 7½-inch rectangles, and two 4 × 12¾-inch rectangles. For the side borders, add one medium blue–and–white Checkerboard unit to each end of the pieced border; see the diagram.

5. Follow the directions in "Adding the Middle and Outer Borders" on page 192 to add the remaining borders, piecing the border strips as necessary.

Large Wallhanging Diagram

6. For the backing, cut the backing fabric in half crosswise. Cut 35-inch-wide segments from each of the pieces. Sew the segments together along the long edge, as shown in the **Backing Diagram.** Press the seams open.

Backing Diagram

7. Layer the quilt top, batting, and backing, and baste the layers together. Use the suggestions in "Quilting and Finishing" on page 193 to choose quilting designs, or quilt as desired. Make double-fold binding and sew it to the quilt, following the directions on page 250.

C U T T I N G

FABRIC	Used For	First Cut		Second Cut			Third Cut	
		Strip Width	No. to Cut	Shape	Dimensions	No. to Cut	Shape	Total No. Needed
Assorted green prints	Strip Sets 1, 2, and 3	2¼"	10	—	—	—	—	—
	Inner border	2¼"	2	—	—	—	—	—
Light blue print	Inner border	2¼"	1	—	—	—	—	—
Medium blue print	Inner border	2¼"	1	—	—	—	—	—
Dark blue print	Middle border	2"	6*	—	—	—	—	—
Assorted violet prints	Sailboat blocks	3½"	5	▬	3½" × 10½"	13	—	—
Assorted orange prints	Sailboat blocks	7¾"	2	▭	7¾" × 5½"	13	—	—
Multicolor print	Outer border	6½"	7	—	—	—	—	—
White print	Strip Set 2	2¼"	6	—	—	—	—	—
	Strip Set 3	4"	4	—	—	—	—	—
	Strip Set 1	5¾"	2	—	—	—	—	—
	Piece 2	3½"	3	▭	3½" × 7¾"	13	—	—
	Piece 3	7¼"	5	▭	7¼" × 11"	13	—	—
	Pieces 5 and 6	4½"	2	□	4½" × 4½"	13	◹	26
	Inner border	2¼"	4	—	—	—	—	—
	Inner border	4"	2	▭	4" × 7½"	8	—	—
	Inner border	4"	2	▭	4" × 12¾"	4	—	—
Binding fabric	Binding	2¼"	7	—	—	—	—	—

*Piece strips together as necessary, then cut borders to length required.

Work a Little Color Magic

Eliminating the Fade Factor

A pile of finished quilts is quite an accomplishment, and keeping them clean and bright can be a challenge. Fabrics, battings, and thread should be kept at a comfortable room temperature at all times. Sunlight, heat, moisture, and dirt can fade color and damage a quilt's fibers in just a few months.

If displaying a quilt on a wall or a sofa, install window treatments that filter light and lessen the chance of sunlight-induced fading and disintegration. It's best if the quilt is in a low-light room, away from high traffic and dirty fingers, and is "rested" every few months.

If you are storing your quilts between seasons or have stacks of completed quilts (good for you!), store your quilts flat on a guest room bed. Cover them with a white sheet so they aren't exposed to light and dust. If you've made the larger version of any of the *Color Magic* quilts and have to fold them for storage, fold each one so that all of the fragile bound edges are contained neatly inside the quilt.

First, lay the quilt flat and fold the two longest sides into the center of the quilt so the edges meet in the middle. Bring the folded edges together to meet in the middle again, then fold the quilt in half once more. In the same manner, fold the top and bottom into the center of the quilt, leaving the edges about 4 to 6 inches apart to accommodate the thickness of the quilt. Bring the folded edges to the center again, then fold in half once more. Slip the folded quilt into a clean, white pillowcase.

Quilts need to be aired out and refolded periodically, every six months or so, to relax the fibers and reduce the stress on any given seam. Try not to stack more than two full-size quilts on top of one another, since it flattens the batting loft and creates a dense, airless environment for the quilts stored at the bottom.

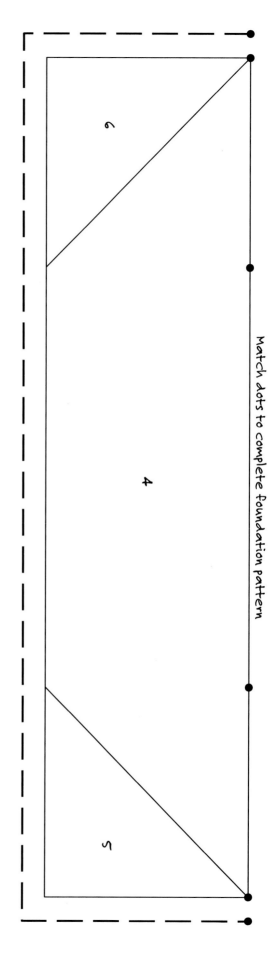

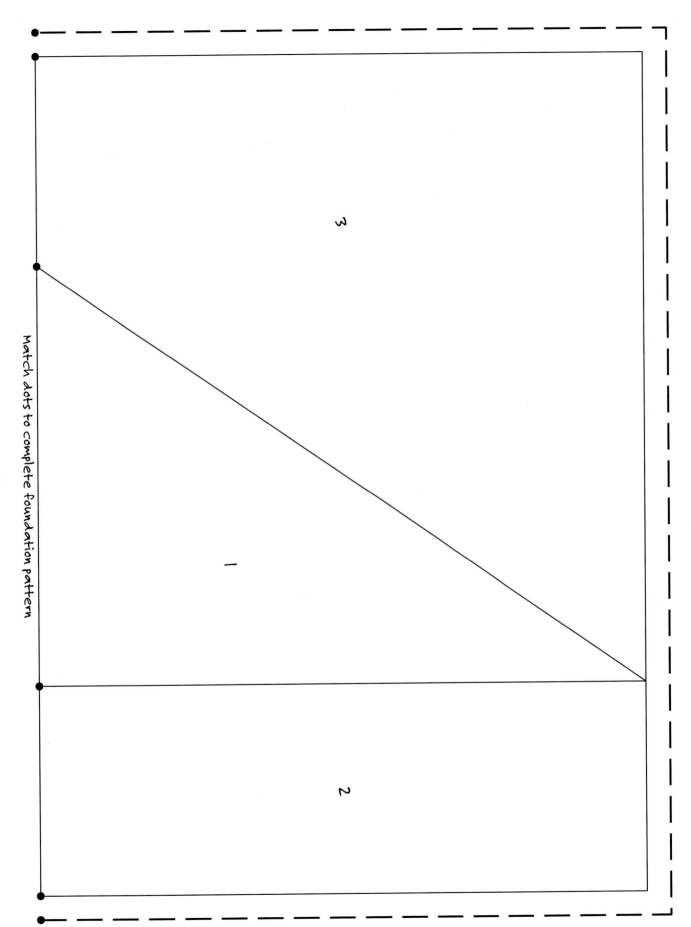

Match dots to complete foundation pattern

3

1

2

Large Wallhanging Block Pattern

Pathways

With a simple value change from light green to dark green and an easy-to-achieve setting, the blocks in this quilt turn the ordinary to extraordinary. The harmony Main Color with Many Colors uses a single color as a unifier, then allows tints and tones of every color to produce a quilt of the prettiest garden variety.

Harmony Featured

Main Color with Many Colors

Colors Used

Green and many colors

MATERIALS

⅝ yard light green solid

⅝ yard dark green solid

½ yard medium green solid

80 assorted light print squares, each 1½ inches

80 assorted dark print squares, each 1½ inches

¼ yard red solid

1⅛ yard backing fabric

⅜ yard binding fabric

35-inch square of quilt batting

SKILL LEVEL: EASY

Finished Quilt Size: 31¼" square

Finished Block Size: 6"

Number of Blocks: 16

Magical Beginnings

The materials list calls for solid fabrics because solid areas of color work best for the "background" in this quilt. While a solid look is the goal, don't limit yourself to true solids. Mottled, marbleized, hand-dyed, and very low contrast print fabrics would also give the same effect.

Dig deep into your scrap bag to find bits and snips of fabric too bright for other projects, and use them for the multicolor squares. The more patterned the fabric is, the more effective it will be. Stay away from tone-on-tone fabrics, since they will only lend color, not texture, to the quilt. All the pieces in this quilt can be quickly rotary cut and pieced. All seam allowances are ¼ inch.

CUTTING

Refer to the chart below and cut the required number of strips. Cut all strips across the crosswise grain, or fabric width.

For the assorted light and dark print squares, cut 1½-inch strips, then subcut the strips into 1½-inch squares if you have larger scraps. If using smaller scraps, cut the fabric directly into squares. You will need eighty 1½-inch light print squares and eighty 1½-inch dark print squares. If you are making the queen-size version of this quilt (page 203), cut 2¼-inch strips, then subcut the strips into 2¼-inch squares. Or cut the fabric directly into squares if you are using scraps. You will need 240 light print squares and 240 dark print squares. **Note:** Cut and piece one sample block before cutting all the quilt fabric.

PIECING THE BLOCKS

There are A blocks and B blocks in this quilt. Both are constructed in exactly the same manner; the placement of the light and dark fabrics in the blocks is the only difference. In the A blocks, assorted light print squares are combined with a dark green solid to form the diagonal pathway; in the B blocks, assorted dark print squares are used with a light green solid to concentrate the dark colors in opposite corners. See the **Block Diagrams.** Each block consists of five Four Patch blocks and four triangle squares.

C U T T I N G

| FABRIC | Used For | First Cut | | Second Cut | | |
		Strip Width	No. to Cut	Shape	Dimensions	No. to Cut
Light green solid	Small squares	1½"	3	⬜	1½" × 1½"	80
	Large squares	2⅞"	3	⬜	2⅞" × 2⅞"	32
Dark green solid	Small squares	1½"	3	⬛	1½" × 1½"	80
	Large squares	2⅞"	3	⬛	2⅞" × 2⅞"	32
Medium green solid	Outer border	3¼"	4	—	—	—
Assorted light prints	Multicolor squares	See "Cutting" above	—	—	—	—
Assorted dark prints	Multicolor squares	See "Cutting" above	—	—	—	—
Red solid	Inner border	1⅛"	4	—	—	—
Binding fabric	Binding	2½"	4	—	—	—

A   B

Block Diagrams

1. To make the triangle squares, use a pencil or permanent marker to draw a diagonal line from corner to corner on the wrong side of a large light green square, as shown in **Diagram 1.** With right sides together, place the large light green square on top of a large dark green square. Sew along both sides of the diagonal line, using the edge of your presser foot as a ¼-inch guide, or draw a line ¼ inch from each side of the diagonal line.

Diagram 1

HINTS FROM HAZEL

If you need to mark the sewing and cutting lines on the triangles and want to make them easily distinguishable from one another, use different-color pencils or pens to draw the lines. For example, use black for the cutting line and blue for the sewing lines.

2. Using your rotary cutter and ruler, cut the squares apart on the drawn diagonal line, as shown in **Diagram 2.** Carefully press the triangle square open, pressing the seam toward the

dark green. Trim off the triangle points at the seam ends. You will get two triangle squares from each pair of squares sewn and cut in this manner.

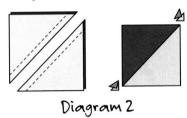

Diagram 2

3. Repeat Steps 1 and 2 for a total of 64 triangle squares.

4. To make the Four Patch blocks, place right sides together and sew a small light green square to a dark print square, as shown in **Diagram 3.** Press the seam toward the dark print. Repeat to make a total of 80 light green units.

Diagram 3

5. With right sides together and the light green fabrics diagonally opposite each other, sew two light green units together, as shown in **Diagram 4.** Press the seam to one side. Repeat to make a total of 40 light green Four Patch blocks.

Diagram 4

6. Repeat Steps 4 and 5 with the dark green and light print squares to make a total of 40 dark green Four Patch blocks.

7. Lay out five Four Patch blocks and four triangle squares in three rows, as shown in **Diagram 5.** Pay close attention to the color patterning and to how the blocks and triangle squares are positioned to form the diagonal pattern in each block. Sew the blocks into rows. Press the seams toward the triangle squares.

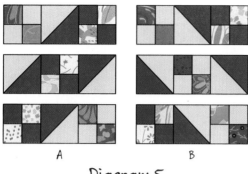

A   B

Diagram 5

8. Sew the rows together, matching seams carefully. In the A blocks, press the seams toward the top of the block. In the B blocks, press the seams toward the bottom of the block.

9. Repeat Steps 7 and 8 for a total of eight A blocks and eight B blocks.

ASSEMBLING THE QUILT

1. Referring to the **Assembly Diagram,** lay out the completed blocks in four rows of four blocks each, paying close attention to the placement of the A and B blocks and the way each is oriented within a row.

Assembly Diagram

Work a Little Color Magic

Avoiding Fabric Bleeds

As soon as you buy new yardage, rinse it in a large sink to remove the sizing. Then soak the fabric in cool water overnight in the sink or the washing machine. Check the water in the morning to see if there is any color in the water. If not, squeeze out the excess water and tumble dry. If you notice that the fabric has bled, change the water and soak it again overnight. Usually, one or two nights of soaking will remove the excess dye; with hand-dyed or color-intense fabrics, however, this process may need to be repeated five or six times. But once the soaking water is clear, you can feel safe that the fabric will not run when used in your quilt.

2. With right sides together, sew the blocks together in horizontal rows, matching seams carefully. Press the seam allowances in opposite directions from row to row.

3. With right sides together, sew the four rows of blocks together, matching seams carefully. Press the seam allowances toward the bottom edge of the quilt.

ADDING THE BORDERS

1. Attach the top and bottom inner borders first. Measure the width of the quilt top, taking the measurement through the horizontal center of the quilt. Cut two inner border strips this exact length.

2. Fold one of the inner border strips in half crosswise, and crease. Unfold it and position it right side down along the top of the quilt, with the crease at the vertical midpoint. Pin at the midpoint and ends first, then along the length of the entire edge, easing in fullness as necessary. Sew the border to the quilt. Repeat for the bottom border. Press seams toward the borders.

3. Measure the length of the quilt, taking the measurement through the vertical center of the quilt and including the top and bottom borders. Cut two inner border strips this exact length.

4. Fold one strip in half crosswise, and crease. Unfold it and position it right side down along one side of the quilt, with the crease at the horizontal midpoint. Pin at the midpoint and ends first, then along the length of the entire side, easing in fullness as necessary. Sew the border to the quilt top. Repeat on the opposite side of the quilt. Press seams toward the border.

5. Prepare and add the outer borders to the quilt in the same manner as for the inner borders, sewing on the top and bottom borders first, then adding the side borders.

QUILTING AND FINISHING

1. Mark quilting designs as desired. The blocks in this quilt were handquilted ¼ inch outside the diagonal "stepping" squares in each block in a continuous line. A twirling ribbon design was handquilted in the outer border.

2. Cut a 35-inch square of backing fabric.

3. Layer the quilt top, batting, and backing, and baste the layers together. Quilt as desired.

4. Make double-fold binding and sew it to the quilt, following the directions on page 250.

Happy Endings

It's always fun to know a little history about the quilt pattern you're using, and the block used for this quilt has a story to tell. More often than not, a quilt block's name is a reflection of events that happened around the time the block was designed or gained popularity. Current events, whether local or national, often influenced everyday life by defining social trends and expanding a person's world view. This block is known by a variety of names that do indeed reflect a particular time period. From the Railroad, Road to California, Off to San Francisco, and Going to Chicago to the Trail of the Covered Wagon, Wagon Tracks, Underground Railroad, and Pacific Railroad, each documented name can be traced to a piece of Americana. There are countless other names for this block as well, but the thread that ties these historical names together is woven strongly through the 1800s.

Queen-Size Quilt

Finished Quilt Size: 83" × 104" **Finished Block Size: 10½"** **Number of Blocks: 48**

MATERIALS

2¾ yards light green solid

2¾ yards dark green solid

3¼ yards medium green solid

240 assorted light print squares, each 2¼ inches

240 assorted dark print squares, each 2¼ inches

⅝ yard red solid

9⅜ yards backing fabric

⅞ yard binding fabric

91 × 112-inch piece of quilt batting

C U T T I N G

FABRIC	Used For	First Cut		Second Cut		
		Strip Width	No. to Cut	Shape	Dimensions	No. to Cut
Light green solid	Small squares	2¼"	14	▢	2¼" × 2¼"	240
	Large squares	4⅜"	11	▢	4⅜" × 4⅜"	96
Dark green solid	Small squares	2¼"	14	◼	2¼" × 2¼"	240
	Large squares	4⅜"	11	◼	4⅜" × 4⅜"	96
Medium green solid	Outer border	9¼"*	4	—	—	—
Assorted light prints	Multicolor squares	See "Cutting" on p. 200	—	—	—	—
Assorted dark prints	Multicolor squares	See "Cutting" on p. 200	—	—	—	—
Red solid	Inner border	1¾"	7	—	—	—
Binding fabric	Binding	2¼"	10	—	—	—

*Cut lengthwise to avoid seams.

DIRECTIONS

1. Read the Pathways project for color and fabric information, basic directions, and helpful tips.

2. Follow the directions in "Piecing the Blocks" on page 200 to make 48 blocks.

3. Lay out the Pathways blocks in eight rows of six blocks each.

4. Follow the directions in "Assembling the Quilt" and "Adding the Borders" on page 202, piecing the border strips as necessary, to assemble the quilt top.

5. For the backing, cut the backing fabric crosswise into three equal pieces, and trim the selvages. Cut 26-inch-wide segments from two of the pieces. Sew one segment to each side of the full-width piece, as shown in the **Backing Diagram**. Press the seams open.

Backing Diagram

6. Layer the quilt top, batting, and backing, and baste the layers together. Quilt as desired. Make double-fold binding and sew it to the quilt, following the directions on page 250.

HINTS FROM HAZEL

Try machine quilting! Use a lightweight nylon thread in the needle. Use a cotton thread in the bobbin in a color that matches the quilt backing.

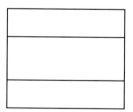

Night Crystals

The dramatic presentation of bright color on black is perfectly suited to the harmony Every Other Color. Vibrant primary and secondary colors make even more of a statement when solid fabrics are used. Commonly recognized as crayonbox colors, red, orange, yellow, green, blue, and violet bring a splash of life to the Mixed T block.

Harmony Featured

Every Other Color

Colors Used

Red, orange, yellow, green, blue, violet

MATERIALS

¼ yard red solid

¼ yard orange solid

¼ yard yellow solid

¼ yard green solid

¼ yard blue solid

¼ yard violet solid

1 yard black print

½ yard multicolor print

1 yard backing fabric

½ yard striped binding fabric

32-inch square of quilt batting

SKILL LEVEL: INTERMEDIATE

Finished Quilt Size: 28" square

Finished Block Size: 4½"

Number of Blocks: 16

Magical Beginnings

To simplify the directions, triangle squares are used instead of a combination of triangle squares and Flying Geese templates, making the seam lines slightly different from the sample quilt. The sample quilt also used two shades of a single color in most instances. The directions, however, have been changed to include yardage for just one shade. All seam allowances are ¼ inch.

CUTTING

All measurements include a ¼-inch seam allowance. Referring to the chart, cut the required number of strips for your quilt. Some strips are only cut once, so no additional cutting information will appear under "Second Cut" or "Third Cut." Cut all strips across the crosswise grain or fabric width. **Note:** Cut and piece one sample block before cutting all the fabric for the quilt.

C U T T I N G

FABRIC	Used For	First Cut Strip Width	First Cut No. to Cut	Second Cut Shape	Second Cut Dimensions	Second Cut No. to Cut	Third Cut Shape	Total No. Needed
Red solid	Small triangles	2⅜"	1	■	2⅜" × 2⅜"	8	◩	15
	Large triangles	3⅞"	1	■	3⅞" × 3⅞"	2	◩	3
Orange solid	Small triangles	2⅜"	1	■	2⅜" × 2⅜"	8	◩	15
	Large triangles	3⅞"	1	■	3⅞" × 3⅞"	2	◩	3
Yellow solid	Small triangles	2⅜"	1	▢	2⅜" × 2⅜"	5	◩	10
	Large triangles	3⅞"	1	▢	3⅞" × 3⅞"	1	◩	2
Green solid	Small triangles	2⅜"	1	■	2⅜" × 2⅜"	8	◩	15
	Large triangles	3⅞"	1	■	3⅞" × 3⅞"	2	◩	3
Blue solid	Small triangles	2⅜"	1	■	2⅜" × 2⅜"	5	◩	10
	Large triangles	3⅞"	1	■	3⅞" × 3⅞"	1	◩	2
Violet solid	Small triangles	2⅜"	1	■	2⅜" × 2⅜"	8	◩	15
	Large triangles	3⅞"	1	■	3⅞" × 3⅞"	2	◩	3
Black print	Small triangles	2⅜"	3	■	2⅜" × 2⅜"	40	◩	80
	Vertical sashing	1½"	1	▬	1½" × 9"	2	—	—
	Horizontal sashing	1½"	1	▬	1½" × 19½"	1	—	—
	Inner border	2"	3	—	—	—	—	—
	Outer border	2½"	4	—	—	—	—	—
Multicolor print	Large triangles	3⅞"	1	▣	3⅞" × 3⅞"	8	◪	16
	Middle border	1½"	4	—	—	—	—	—

PIECING THE BLOCKS

1. Sew a small green triangle to a small black triangle to form a triangle square; see **Diagram 1.** Press the seam toward the green fabric. Repeat to make five green/black triangle squares.

Diagram 1

2. Sew a large green triangle to a large multicolor triangle to form a triangle square; see **Diagram 2.** Press the seam toward the green fabric.

Diagram 2

3. Sew the small triangle squares together in two groups, referring to **Diagram 3.** Press the seam toward the green fabric.

Diagram 3

4. Sew the shorter triangle-square strip to the large triangle square; see **Diagram 4.** Sew the other triangle-square strip to the block. Press the seam toward the large triangle square.

Diagram 4

5. Repeat Steps 1 through 4 to make a total of three red, three orange, two yellow, three green, two blue, and three violet blocks.

ASSEMBLING THE QUILT

1. Use a flat surface to arrange the blocks, vertical sashing strips, and horizontal sashing strips, as shown in the **Assembly Diagram.**

Assembly Diagram

2. With right sides together, sew together each group of four blocks, as shown in the diagram.

3. With right sides together, sew a four-block group to either side of a vertical sashing strip to assemble a row. Press the seams toward the sashing strip. Repeat for the remaining row.

4. Sew the horizontal sashing between the rows. Press the seams toward the sashing.

ADDING THE BORDERS

1. Attach the top and bottom inner borders first. Measure the width of the quilt top, taking the measurement through the horizontal center of the quilt, rather than along the edges. Cut two border strips this exact length.

2. Fold one strip in half crosswise and crease. Unfold it and position it right side down along the top of the quilt, with the crease at the vertical midpoint. Pin at the midpoint and ends first, then along the length of the entire edge, easing in any fullness. Sew the border to the quilt. Repeat for the bottom border. Press the seams toward the borders.

3. Measure the length of the quilt top, taking the measurement through the vertical center of the quilt and including the top and bottom borders. Cut and piece two inner border strips this exact length and sew these to the sides of the quilt, referring to Step 2. Ease in fullness as necessary. Press the seams toward the borders.

4. Repeat Steps 1 through 3 to add the middle and outer borders.

QUILTING AND FINISHING

1. Mark quilting designs as desired. The blocks and inner and middle borders in this quilt were handquilted ⅛ inch away from the seam lines. The inner border was also accented with quilting stitches that mimic the outer edges of the Night Crystals blocks. A zigzag design was handquilted in the outer border.

2. Cut a 32-inch square of backing fabric.

3. Layer the quilt top, batting, and backing, and baste the layers together. Quilt as desired.

Happy Endings

The striped fabric used for the binding was cut on the bias so the full range of colors in the stripes would be visible. The binding was also pieced at set intervals to create a chevron at the center of each side and the corners of the quilt. These directions have been streamlined to create a bias binding that shows off striped fabric without much fuss or as many steps.

Cut 125 inches of 1⅝-inch-wide bias strips. To join the strips, cut each strip end at a 45 degree angle. Place the strips with right sides together, offsetting the tips, as shown. Sew the strips together using a ¼-inch seam allowance, then press the seams open.

Round off the corners of the quilt, using a saucer as a guide. With right sides together, gently lay the binding around the curve, taking care not to stretch the binding as it is positioned. Match the ¼-inch seam line of the binding with the ¼-inch seam line of the quilt, then pin the binding in place, easing in a bit of fullness at the corner. Sew the binding to the quilt, working slowly as you sew through the curve. Flip the binding to the wrong side of the quilt and press under a ¼-inch seam allowance. Hand sew the folded edge of the binding to the back of the quilt.

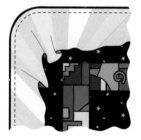

Twin-Size Quilt

Finished Quilt Size: 68½" × 87½"   **Finished Block Size: 7½"**   **Number of Blocks: 35**

MATERIALS

½ yard red solid	½ yard blue solid	5⅞ yards backing fabric
½ yard orange solid	½ yard violet solid	1 yard striped binding fabric
½ yard yellow solid	5½ yards black print	77 × 96-inch piece of quilt batting
½ yard green solid	1⅛ yard multicolor print	

C U T T I N G

FABRIC	Used For	First Cut		Second Cut			Third Cut	
		Strip Width	No. to Cut	Shape	Dimensions	No. to Cut	Shape	Total No. Needed
Red solid	Small triangles	3⅜"	2	■	3⅜" × 3⅜"	15	◩	30
	Large triangles	5⅞"	1	■	5⅞" × 5⅞"	3	◩	6
Orange solid	Small triangles	3⅜"	2	■	3⅜" × 3⅜"	15	◩	30
	Large triangles	5⅞"	1	■	5⅞" × 5⅞"	3	◩	6
Yellow solid	Small triangles	3⅜"	2	□	3⅜" × 3⅜"	15	◩	30
	Large triangles	5⅞"	1	□	5⅞" × 5⅞"	3	◩	6
Green solid	Small triangles	3⅜"	2	■	3⅜" × 3⅜"	15	◩	30
	Large triangles	5⅞"	1	■	5⅞" × 5⅞"	3	◩	6
Blue solid	Small triangles	3⅜"	2	■	3⅜" × 3⅜"	15	◩	30
	Large triangles	5⅞"	1	■	5⅞" × 5⅞"	3	◩	6
Violet solid	Small triangles	3⅜"	2	■	3⅜" × 3⅜"	15	◩	30
	Large triangles	5⅞"	1	■	5⅞" × 5⅞"	3	◩	6
Black print	Outer border	9"*	4	▬	9" × 96"	6	—	—
	Horizontal sashing	2½"*	6	▬	2½" × 46"	6	—	—
	Vertical sashing	2½"†	10	▬	2½" × 8"	28	—	—
	Small triangles	3⅜"†	11	■	3⅜" × 3⅜"	90	◩	180
	Inner border	2½"	6	—	—	—	—	—
Multicolor print	Large triangles	5⅞"	3	▥	5⅞" × 5⅞"	18	◪	36
	Middle border	1½"	7	—	—	—	—	—

*Cut lengthwise to avoid seams.

†Cut these strips crosswise from the remaining width of the fabric cut for the horizontal sashing; see the **Cutting Diagram** on the opposite page.

DIRECTIONS

1. Read the Night Crystals project for color and fabric information, basic directions, and helpful tips and hints.

2. Follow the directions in "Piecing the Blocks" on page 208 to make 36 blocks, 6 each of red, orange, yellow, green, blue, and violet.

3. Lay out the blocks in seven rows of five blocks each, adding the sashing strips between the blocks. Position the various block colors as desired or as shown in the **Twin-Size Assembly Diagram.** In the diagram, the blocks "point" in opposite directions from row to row. The block colors are positioned randomly. You will have one block left over to use as a label.

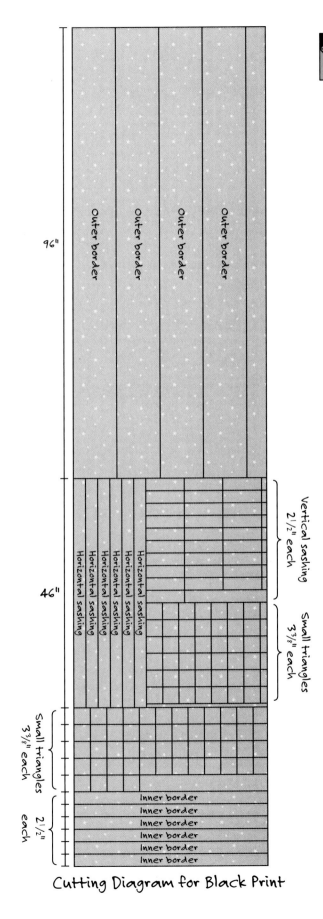

Cutting Diagram for Black Print

(labels within diagram: 96", Outer border, Outer border, Outer border, Outer border, 46", Vertical sashing 2½" each, Small triangles 3⅜" each, Horizontal sashing, Small triangles 3⅜" each, Inner border 2½" each)

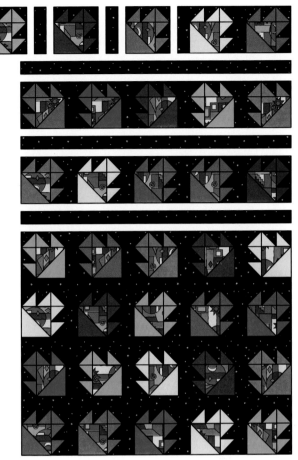

Twin-Size Assembly Diagram

4. Follow the directions in "Assembling the Quilt" and "Adding the Borders" on page 208 to assemble the quilt top, piecing the inner borders.

5. For the backing, cut the backing fabric in half crosswise, and trim the selvages. Cut 18-inch-wide segments from one of the pieces. Sew one segment to each side of the full-width piece; see the **Backing Diagram.** Press the seams open.

Backing Diagram

6. Layer the quilt top, batting, and backing; baste. Quilt as desired. Make 327 inches of bias binding as directed on page 209, and sew it to the quilt.

Garden Maze

Inspired by the Colourwash style of English quiltmaker Deirdre Amsden, a painterly selection of lights, mediums, and darks is transformed into a quilt blooming with color. Trace your finger along the garden's perimeter and see how many colors of the color wheel are represented in fabric squares. Then peer over the tall, dark "hedgerows" typical of long-ago England to see the maze of color within.

Harmony Featured

Many Colors

Colors Used

Many colors

MATERIALS

216 assorted medium print 2-inch squares

108 assorted dark print 2-inch squares, including greens, reds, blues, violets, and browns

81 assorted light print 2-inch squares

36 assorted very dark print 2-inch squares

1⅛ yards backing fabric

⅜ yard binding fabric

35-inch square of quilt batting

SKILL LEVEL: EASY

Finished Quilt Size: 31½" square

Finished Size of Squares: 1½"

Number of Squares: 441

Magical Beginnings

Successful colorwash quilts combine hundreds of fabrics in different colors and values. The Garden Maze quilt uses fabrics in four values: lights, mediums, darks, and very darks. The lights are light fabrics that feature soft pastel colors on neutral backgrounds. The mediums are floral pastels with a medium-print scale. The darks are dark brights with a lot of pattern. The very darks are low-contrast black prints with a hint of color. When assembling this quilt, use ¼-inch seam allowances.

CUTTING

The yardage in the materials list is the minimum you'll need for the assorted fabrics. When creating watercolor quilts, have a variety of multicolor fabrics at your fingertips. Use small scraps of fabric for a larger selection. It's a good idea to cut more squares than required of each value so you'll have a greater choice of color and print when arranging the maze pattern.

C U T T I N G

	First Cut		
FABRIC	**Shape**	**Dimensions**	**Total No. Needed**
Lights	☐	2" × 2"	81
Mediums	◻	2" × 2"	216
Darks	◼	2" × 2"	108
Very darks	■	2" × 2"	36

	First Cut	
FABRIC	**Strip Width**	**No. to Cut**
Binding fabric	2¼"	4

PLANNING

Keep your fabrics separated by value as you work. You may find that you can move some fabrics

to a different value group depending on where they fall in the design. Sort the dark fabrics by color since the "hedgerows" in the maze are most effective when the colors blend from one into another.

1. Using the **Value Placement Diagrams,** lay out the fabric squares in the maze pattern. These diagrams are representations of the Garden Maze quilt and should be used as loose guidelines for color placement. When laying out squares, be sure to place similar-color fabrics next to each other within a value area for continuity. This area of concentrated color should gently blend into neighboring fabrics to create a colorwash look. Try not to use more than five squares of any one fabric unless you have a special purpose in mind, such as the very dark squares in the center of the maze. Be sure that the contrast of fabrics weaving over and under the maze is strong enough to create a three-dimensional effect.

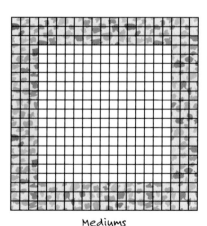

Lights

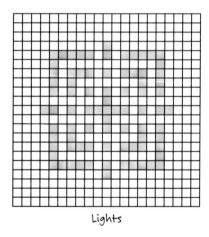

Mediums

Value Placement Diagrams

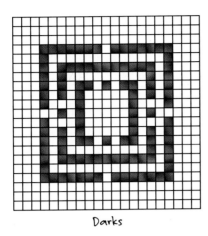

Darks

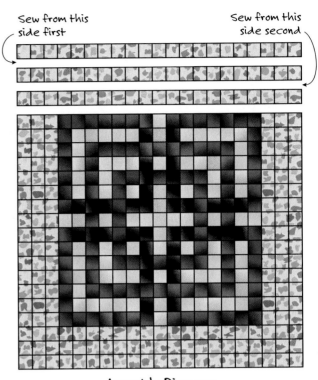

Sew from this side first

Sew from this side second

Assembly Diagram

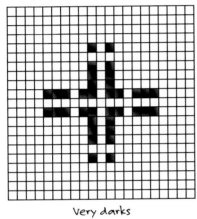

Very darks

Value Placement Diagrams

2. Using a design wall can be very helpful for colorwash quilts. Keep the quilt on the wall for a few days, spending an hour or so each day rearranging and replacing squares that are too strong, too subtle, or too jarring. Adjust the squares and colors in your quilt as necessary to create the most effective design. Try to place the squares right next to each other on the wall, preventing the background from showing through and altering the overall colorwash effect.

PIECING THE QUILT

1. Sew the squares into rows. Press the seam allowances in alternate directions from row to row.

2. Alternating the side that you begin sewing, sew the rows together, taking care to match seams; see the **Assembly Diagram.** Press the quilt top.

QUILTING AND FINISHING

1. Mark quilting designs as desired. From the maze area inward, each block in this quilt was handquilted in the ditch. A meandering, cloud-like continuous line was quilted in the outer "border" to accentuate the softness of the floral fabrics.

2. Cut a 35-inch square of backing fabric.

3. Layer the quilt top, batting, and backing, and baste the layers together. Quilt as desired.

4. Make double-fold binding and sew it to the quilt, following the directions on page 250.

Happy Endings

Just as Monet, Manet, and Renoir have done, you have created an impressionistic work of art. Make space for a gallery in your living room or foyer of small colorwash quilts, using Garden Maze as the focal point.

Autumn Glow

As summer fades into fall and days grow shorter, mariners spend more time using their navigational instruments since the sun sets so early in the evening. Using the harmony Colors on a Triangle with an Accent, this quilt captures the spirit of a seafarer's compass and the mood of the autumn sky with its precisely pieced points and its rich twilight colors.

MATERIALS

⅛ yard light yellow-orange print
½ yard medium yellow-orange print
¼ yard medium blue-green print
⅛ yard dark blue-green print
⅛ yard medium red-violet print
⅛ yard dark red-violet print
⅛ yard light yellow-green print
⅛ yard medium yellow-green print
¾ yard black print
⅞ yard cream print
⅞ yard backing fabric
⅜ yard binding fabric
29-inch square of quilt batting

SKILL LEVEL: ADVANCED
Finished Quilt Size: 24½" square
Finished Medallion Size: 12"

Magical Beginnings

The Mariner's Compass medallion combines foundation piecing and curved piecing. You will need to prepare four paper foundations each for A and B on pages 226–227; prepare eight paper foundations for the border, using the **One-Half Border Pattern** on page 226. For information on preparing foundations and paper piecing, refer to page 248.

You will need to make templates for pattern piece C on page 227 for information about making and using templates, see page 247. All seam allowances are ¼ inch unless specified otherwise.

CUTTING

Refer to the chart below and cut the required number of strips and pieces. The cut sizes of the

C U T T I N G

FABRIC	Used For	Strip Width	No. to Cut	Shape	Dimensions	No. to Cut
		First Cut		**Second Cut**		
Light yellow-orange print	Compass points	1½"	1	—	—	—
Medium yellow-orange print	Compass points	1½"	1	—	—	—
	Outer border	3¼"	4	▭	3¼" × 30"	4
Medium blue-green print	Compass points	2"	1	—	—	—
	Middle border	1"	4	▬	1" × 30"	4
Dark blue-green print	Compass points	2"	1	—	—	—
Medium red-violet print	Compass points	2½"	1	—	—	—
Dark red-violet print	Compass points	2½"	1	—	—	—
Light yellow-green print	Compass points	1½"	1	—	—	—
Medium yellow-green print	Compass points	1½"	1	—	—	—
Black print	Pieced border	2¼"	6	—	—	—
	Cornerstones	3½"	1	■	3½" × 3½"	4
	Inner border	1½"	2	▬	1½" × 12½"	4
Cream print	Pieced border	2¼"	6	—	—	—
	Compass background	3¼"	2	—	—	—
	C	C pieces	4	—	—	—
Binding fabric	Binding	2½"	3	—	—	—

rectangular fabric strips for paper piecing include generous seam allowances. With the foundation method, it's easier to work with wider strips when you are first learning the technique and especially when you are paper piecing triangular shapes. You may wish to decrease the width of the strips by ⅛-inch increments as you become more familiar with this technique. Cut all strips across the crosswise grain, or fabric width. **Note:** Cut and piece one sample section before cutting all the fabric for this quilt.

PIECING THE MEDALLION

The Mariner's Compass medallion is paper pieced in eight sections, four each of A and B. Each paper-pieced section contains compass point fabric and background fabrics. See the **Medallion Diagrams** for color placement for the A and B sections. Once the paper piecing is completed, the paper-pieced sections are sewn together in sets of two to create a wedge. The wedges are then joined with a cream C piece to create one-quarter of the medallion.

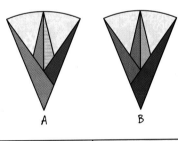

Medallion Diagrams

1. Fabric strips are positioned on the back, or unmarked, side of the foundation. Strips are added in numerical order starting at 1. All sewing takes place on the front side of the foundation, directly on the drawn lines. All lines on the foundation, except the dashed one around the outer perimeter, are seam lines. These steps illustrate making an A foundation. To begin, layer a light yellow-orange compass point strip on top of a medium yellow-orange compass point strip, with right sides together. Position these strips underneath one of the paper piecing foundations, so that the medium yellow-orange strip lies against the paper foundation, as shown in **Diagram 1.** The edges of the strips must extend at least ¼ inch beyond the seam line between 1 and 2 on the paper foundation to ensure a stable seam allowance, as shown. Making 12 to 14 stitches per inch, sew on the line separating 1 and 2, beginning and ending the stitching approximately ¼ inch on either side of the line, as shown.

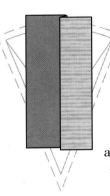

Diagram 1

2. Flip the light yellow-orange strip into a right-side-up position, pressing it firmly in place, as shown in **Diagram 2.** Hold the foundation up to the light with the paper side toward you. You will now be able to see the shadow created by the light yellow-orange fabric. The shadow should overlap all lines drawn for compass point 2, and the overlap should be sufficient to create a stable seam allowance. If it is not, use a seam ripper to remove the background from the foundation, then reposition the piece and try again. This ensures that there will be enough seam allowance on all sides when you add the adjacent fabric strips.

Diagram 2

3. Referring to **Diagram 3,** place a cream print compass background strip right sides together with the 1 and 2 pieces. It may be helpful to pin the loose edge of piece 1 to the foundation to keep it flat while stitching the next strip. Be sure the new background strip extends at least ¼ inch beyond the seam line between 1 and 3, then sew along this seam line.

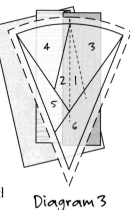

Diagram 3

4. To minimize bulk with overlapping the seam allowances, trim fabrics to a scant ¼ inch beyond the seam line between 1 and 3, as shown in **Diagram 4;** be sure to fold the foundation paper away from the fabric to avoid cutting it while you trim the seam allowance.

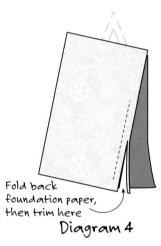

Fold back foundation paper, then trim here

Diagram 4

5. Flip the compass background piece into a right-side-up position, pressing it firmly in place, as shown in **Diagram 5.** If you prefer, keep an iron near your work area to press pieces as you go. It's best to avoid using steam because it tends to wrinkle the foundation paper.

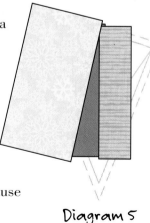

Diagram 5

6. Add compass background 4 in the same manner as compass background 3 in Step 3;

see **Diagram 6.** Trim the seam allowance to a scant ¼ inch to minimize bulk with overlapping seam allowances. Flip the background into a right-side-up position and press it firmly in place in the same manner as described in Step 5.

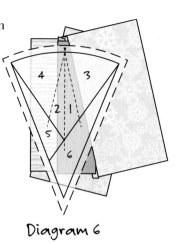

Diagram 6

7. Add compass point 5 to the foundation, using a dark blue-green strip, as shown in **Diagram 7.** Flip the compass point into a right-side-up position and press it firmly in place.

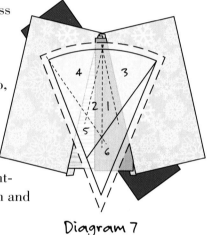

Diagram 7

8. Add compass point 6, using a medium red-violet strip, as shown in **Diagram 8.** Flip the compass point into a right-side-up position and press it firmly in place.

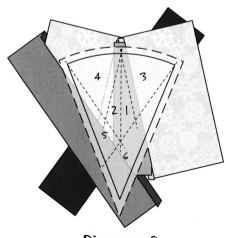

Diagram 8

220

9. Trim the edges of the fabric strips even with the dashed line on the foundation paper. Do not remove the paper foundation at this time.

10. Repeat Steps 1 through 9 to make a total of four A foundations.

11. Repeat Steps 1 through 9 to make a total of four B foundations, using fabric colors as shown in the **Medallion Diagrams** on page 219.

ASSEMBLING THE MEDALLION

1. With right sides together, sew an A foundation to a B foundation along the blue-green compass points to create one-quarter of the compass; see **Diagram 9.** Press the seam allowance toward the B foundation.

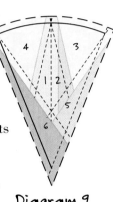

Diagram 9

2. Repeat Step 1 to join the three remaining quarter-compasses.

3. Crease the midpoints of the curve of a quarter-compass and a C piece. Make a few ⅛-inch clips into the concave (inward) seam allowance of the C piece. With the C piece on top, place the right sides of the curved edges together, matching the beginnings, midpoints, and ends. Pin generously, then sew the quarter-compass and C together; see **Diagram 10.** Press the seam toward C. This square forms one-quarter of the medallion.

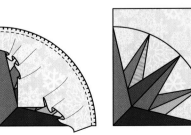

Diagram 10

4. In the same manner, sew the remaining quarter-compasses and the C pieces together to create square blocks, clipping the paper foundation as necessary to ease in any fullness.

5. Lay out the quarter-medallion blocks in two rows, matching the compass points to create a circular Mariner's Compass pattern.

6. Sew the top row of blocks together. Press the seam toward A. Repeat for the bottom row. Sew the rows together to create the center medallion. Press the seam toward the bottom of the quilt. Remove the paper foundation.

7. Using a rotary ruler and cutter, trim the completed center medallion to 12½ inches square.

HINTS FROM HAZEL

While it may not be practical to have every type and size of rotary ruler made, it would be helpful to have at least one large-size square ruler to trim blocks once they're assembled. Both the 12½-inch square ruler and the 15-inch square ruler are good choices and are more versatile than the smaller square rulers. Use a large-size ruler on this project to trim the medallion to 12½ inches square.

PIECING THE BORDER

The inner border has three components—the pieced border, the inner border strip, and the cornerstone. The pieced border is paper pieced with two fabrics—the black print and the cream print. Use the black print for the odd-numbered triangles and the cream print for the even-numbered ones.

1. To create one 12-inch-long border foundation, tape two **One-Half Border Patterns** together; see **Diagram 11.** Half-triangle 13 and half-triangle 1 merge to create a whole triangle.

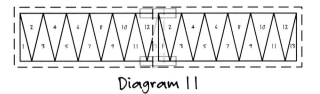

Diagram 11

2. Using the same methods described in "Piecing the Medallion" on page 219, layer a black print strip and a cream print strip with right sides together. Position these strips underneath one of the border foundations so that the black print strip lies against the foundation, as shown in **Diagram 12.** Sew on the line separating 1 and 2, as shown. Flip the cream print strip into a right-side-up position, finger pressing it firmly in place.

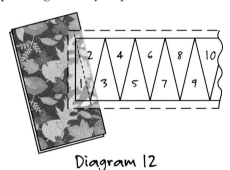

Diagram 12

3. Position and sew a black print strip right sides together with the 1 and 2 pieces, extending the new strip ¼ inch beyond the seam line between 2 and 3; see **Diagram 13.**

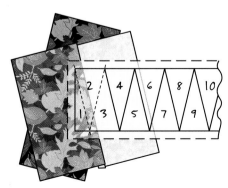

Diagram 13

4. Trim fabrics to a scant ¼ inch beyond the seam line, folding the foundation paper away from the fabric to avoid cutting it.

5. Repeat Steps 2 through 4 to complete a pieced border. Make a total of four pieced borders.

ADDING THE PIECED BORDER

1. With right sides together, sew an inner border strip to a pieced border; see **Diagram 14.** Press the seam toward the inner border strip. Repeat for a total of four inner border units.

Diagram 14

2. Referring to the **Assembly Diagram,** sew one inner border unit to each side of the medallion. Press the seams toward the medallion. Sew one cornerstone to either end of the two remaining inner border units, then sew one assembled unit to the top and bottom of the medallion. Press the seams toward the medallion.

Assembly Diagram

3. Remove the paper foundations from the borders.

ADDING THE OUTER BORDERS

1. With right sides together, sew a middle border to an outer border. Treat the borders as one unit. Press the seams toward the outer border. Repeat to make four borders.

Sorting Your Stash

Take the time every few months to sort your fabrics. If you don't have closet or shelf space, consider stackable baskets or bins to keep things organized. Using the color wheel as a starting point for sorting, separate the reds, oranges, yellows, greens, blues, and violets from your stash. Once these colors are grouped, narrow each category one step further. Put the red-violets in one basket, the red-reds in another, and the red-oranges in a third one. You may be surprised at how many blended-color fabrics you have acquired on your shopping sprees and how few pure color fabrics you have. Continue sorting until you have all 12 color wheel fabrics in separate baskets.

Blacks, grays, whites, creams, and other neutrals should also be sorted into separate baskets. And you'll probably need a basket for those fabrics that refuse to have a main color or ones that are so multicolored that they can't be easily categorized.

You may find that some fabrics actually fit into two different places, so it's really a matter of personal preference where they're stored. Sorting is a fun way to spend a blustery afternoon—you'll not only develop color identification skills, but you'll also finish the day with a neat and tidy sewing room.

2. Read "Mitered Borders" on pages 248–249. Make the 45 degree angle cuts and mark the ¼-inch seam intersections as directed. Repeat for all four borders. Find the center of each border by folding it in half and marking the midpoint with a pin. Find the center of each quilt side by folding and marking with a pin. With right sides together, pin each border to the quilt, beginning at the center. Pin at each ¼-inch seam intersection, then generously pin the remaining areas, easing in any fullness. Sew each border to the quilt, stopping and starting at the marked ¼-inch seam intersections.

3. Miter the corner seams, referring to page 249 for details.

QUILTING AND FINISHING

1. Mark quilting designs as desired. The Mariner's Compass points in this quilt were handquilted in the ditch. Large triangular shapes were handquilted in the cream area of the Mariner's Compass and in the paper-pieced border. A diamond-shaped cable was quilted in the outer border.

2. Cut a 29-inch square of backing fabric.

3. Layer the quilt top, batting, and backing, and baste the layers together. Quilt as desired.

4. Make double-fold binding, and sew it to the quilt, following the directions on page 250.

Happy Endings

With another finished project to admire, take some time to clean up your sewing space or sewing room. Sort the scraps left from your paper piecing and toss out those pieces too small to reuse. Empty your waste paper basket, clean the soleplate on your iron, and corral the dust bunnies under your sewing table. Put in a new sewing machine needle, change your rotary cutter blade, and wind a few bobbins so you're ready to go as soon as inspiration strikes again.

Large Wallhanging

Finished Quilt Size: 53½" square   **Finished Medallion Size: 12"**   **Number of Medallions: 9**

MATERIALS

⅜ yard light yellow-orange print

2 yards medium yellow-orange print

⅞ yard medium blue-green print

½ yard dark blue-green print

¾ yard medium red-violet print

¾ yard dark red-violet print

⅜ yard light yellow-green print

⅜ yard medium yellow-green print

1½ yards black print

4¼ yards cream print

3⅜ yards backing fabric

½ yard binding fabric

62-inch square of quilt batting

DIRECTIONS

1. Read the Autumn Glow project for color and fabric information, basic assembly directions, and helpful tips.

2. Prepare 36 paper foundations each for A and B on pages 226–227; prepare 24 paper foundations for the border, using the **One-Half Border Pattern** on page 226.

3. Follow the directions in "Piecing the Medallion" and "Assembling the Medallion" on pages 219–221 to make nine Mariner's Compass medallions.

4. Lay out the quilt in three rows of three blocks each. Sew the blocks into rows, then sew the rows together.

5. Follow the directions in "Piecing the Border" on page 221 to make the four pieced borders; tape six **One-Half Border Patterns** together to create each border foundation.

6. To attach the borders, follow the directions in "Adding the Pieced Border" and "Adding the Outer Borders" on pages 222–223.

Large Wallhanging Diagram

7. For the backing, cut the backing fabric in half crosswise and trim the selvages. Cut 31-inch-wide segments from each of the pieces. Sew the segments together along the long edge, as shown in the **Backing Diagram** on the next page. Press the seams open. Position the backing with the seam in either the vertical or horizontal direction.

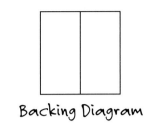

Backing Diagram

8. To complete the quilt, follow the directions in "Quilting and Finishing" on page 223.

9. Because of the size of this wallhanging, you may want a second hanging sleeve at the bottom. Insert a dowel into the sleeve to prevent curling.

C U T T I N G

FABRIC	Used For	Strip Width	No. to Cut	Shape	Dimensions	No. to Cut
		First Cut		Second Cut		
Light yellow-orange print	Compass points	1½"	5	—	—	—
Medium yellow-orange print	Outer border	5½"*	4	▬	5½" × 58"	4
	Compass points	1½"†	9	—	—	—
Medium blue-green print	Middle border	1¼"‡	4	▬	1¼" × 58"	4
	Compass points	2"	7	—	—	—
Dark blue-green print	Compass points	2"	5	—	—	—
Medium red-violet print	Compass points	2½"	8	—	—	—
Dark red-violet print	Compass points	2½"	8	—	—	—
Light yellow-green print	Compass points	1½"	5	—	—	—
Medium yellow-green print	Compass points	1½"	5	—	—	—
Black print	Pieced border	2¼"	16	—	—	—
	Cornerstones	3½"	1	■	3½" × 3½"	4
	Inner border	1½"	4	▬	1½" × 36½"	4
Cream print	Pieced border	2¼"	16	—	—	—
	Compass background	3¼"	16	—	—	—
	C	C pieces	36	—	—	—
Binding fabric	Binding	2½"	6	—	—	—

*Cut lengthwise to avoid seams.

†Cut these strips crosswise from the remaining width of the fabric cut for the borders.

‡Piece these strips together, then cut into 58-inch lengths.

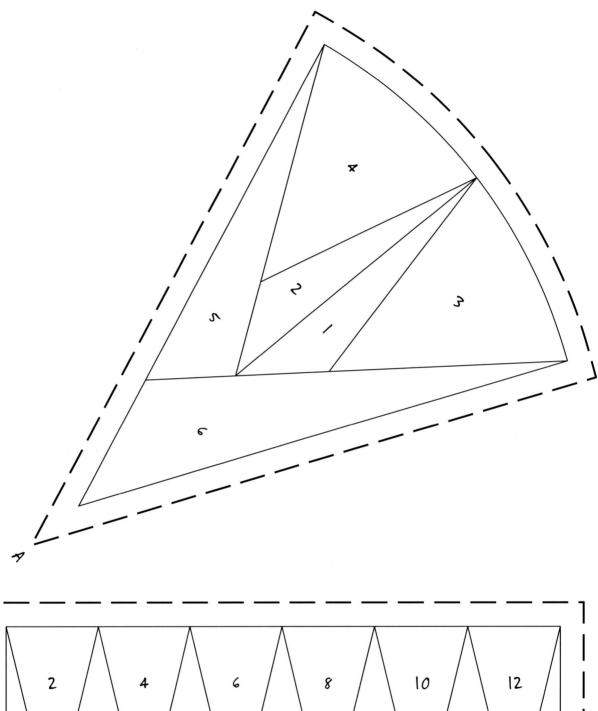

One-Half Border Pattern

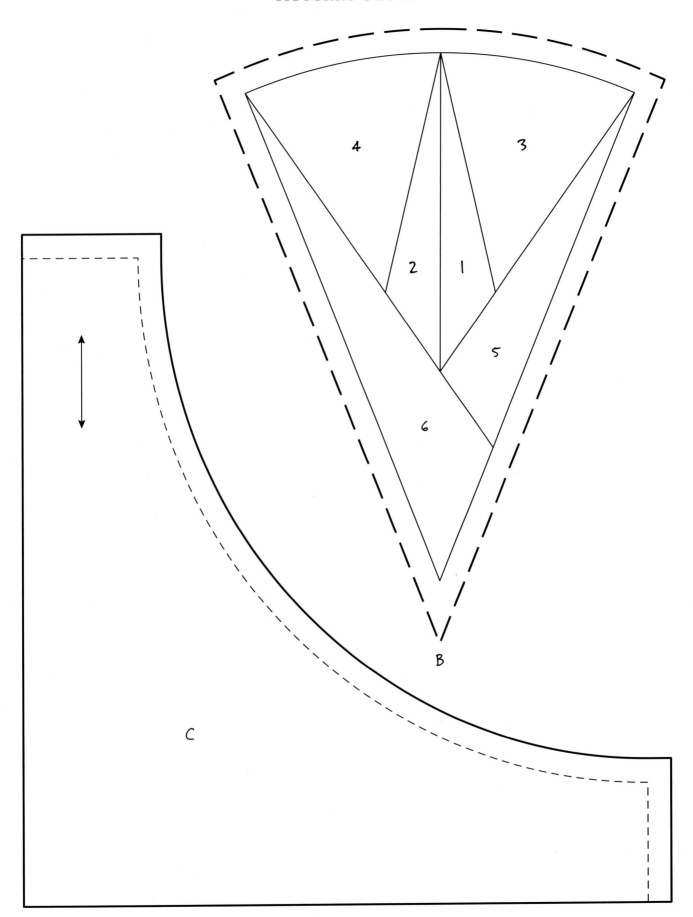

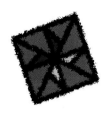

Star Dance

Pirouetting like stars on stage, the carefully planned red-orange and yellow-orange star points form a "border" within a border. Star Dance features a pleasing balance of color temperature and demonstrates the power of combining very warm colors with a cool color— achieved using the harmony Splitting the Opposite.

Harmony Featured

Splitting the Opposite

Colors Used

Blue, red-orange, and yellow-orange

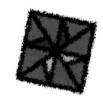

MATERIALS

¾ yard assorted very dark blue prints

⅝ yard assorted medium dark blue prints

½ yard assorted medium blue prints

½ yard light blue print

¼ yard red-orange print

¼ yard light red-orange print

⅜ yard yellow-orange print

¾ yard backing fabric

⅜ yard binding fabric

25-inch square of quilt batting

SKILL LEVEL: EASY

Finished Quilt Size: 21" square

Finished Block Size: 5"

Number of Blocks: 9

Magical Beginnings

To re-create the scrappy look of this quilt, use as many blue fabrics as you can find. Remember to choose very dark blue prints to make the stars shine brightly. Since you only need a small amount of most blues, it may be easier and more cost-effective to buy fat quarters (18 × 20 inches) or fat eighths (9 × 20 inches) for greater variety. Or dig deep into your scrap bag for bits and pieces of various blue prints.

The blocks in this quilt are paper pieced so you will need to prepare two paper foundations for each block, using the **Block Pattern** on page 233. For information on preparing foundations and paper piecing, refer to page 248. All seam allowances are ¼ inch unless specified otherwise.

CUTTING

Refer to the chart below and cut the required number of strips and pieces. Cut all strips across the crosswise grain. The cut sizes of the strips include generous seam allowances. With the foundation method, it's easier to work with wider strips. You may wish to decrease the width of the strips by ⅛-inch increments as you become more familiar with this technique.

Since you will be using a variety of blue prints for the star blocks, you will be cutting single pieces of fabric instead of cutting strips. You will probably only want one or two pieces of each fabric, to create a scrappy look. **Note:** Cut and piece one sample block on a foundation before cutting all the fabric for the quilt.

C U T T I N G

FABRIC	Used For	First Cut		
		Shape	Dimensions	No. to Cut
Assorted very dark blue prints	Star blocks	▬	3" × 4¾"	36
Assorted medium dark blue prints	Star blocks	▬	3" × 3½"	20
Assorted medium blue prints	Star blocks	▬	3" × 3½"	16

FABRIC	Used For	First Cut		Second Cut		
		Strip Width	No. to Cut	Shape	Dimensions	No. to Cut
Light blue print	Outer border	3"	4	▬	3" × 26"	4
Red-orange print	Star blocks	3¼"	1	▬	3¼" × 2½"	12
Light red-orange print	Inner border	1"	4	▬	1" × 26"	4
Yellow-orange print	Star blocks	3¼"	2	▬	3¼" × 2½"	24
Binding fabric	Binding	2½"	3	—	—	—

PIECING THE BLOCKS

The diagrams in the directions illustrate the fabric colors used in the A block. Use the same piecing method for the B and C blocks; just substitute the colors shown in the **Block Diagrams** for those shown here.

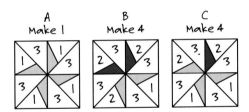

Block Diagrams

FABRIC KEY
1 Medium blue prints
2 Medium dark blue prints
3 Very dark blue prints

1. Fabric strips are positioned on the back, or unmarked, side of the foundation. Strips are added in numerical order starting at 1. All sewing takes place on the front side, directly on the drawn lines. All lines on the foundation, except the dashed one around the outer perimeter, are seam lines. To begin, lay piece 1 on top of piece 2 with right sides together. Position these pieces underneath one of the paper piecing foundations, so that piece 1 lies against the paper foundation, as shown in **Diagram 1.** The edges of the pieces must extend ¼ inch beyond the seam line between 1 and 2 on the paper foundation, as shown. Making 12 to 14 stitches per inch, sew on the line separating 1 and 2, beginning and ending the stitching approximately ¼ inch on either side of the line, as shown.

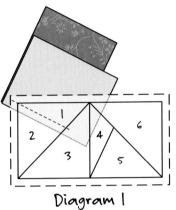

Diagram 1

2. Flip piece 2 into a right-side-up position, pressing it in place; see **Diagram 2.** Hold the foundation up to the light with the paper side toward you. You will now be able to see the shadow created by piece 2. The shadow should overlap all lines drawn for piece 2, and the overlap should be sufficient to create a stable seam allowance. If it is not, use a seam ripper to remove piece 2 from the foundation, then reposition the piece and try again. This ensures that there will be enough seam allowance on all sides when you add the adjacent fabric pieces.

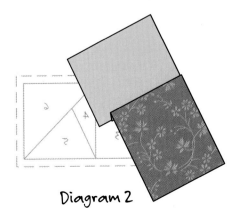

Diagram 2

3. Referring to **Diagram 3,** place piece 3 right sides together with the 1 and 2 pieces. It may be helpful to pin the loose edges of pieces 1 and 2 to the foundation to avoid lumps when adding the next strip. Be sure piece 3 extends at least ¼ inch beyond the seam line between 2 and 3, then sew along this seam line.

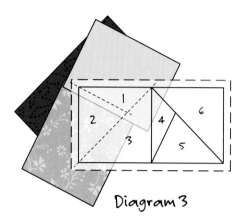

Diagram 3

4. Trim pieces 2 and 3 to a scant ¼ inch beyond the seam line between 2 and 3, as shown in **Diagram 4;** be sure to fold the foundation paper away from the fabric to avoid cutting it as you trim the seam allowance. Flip piece 3 into a right-side-up position, pressing it firmly in place.

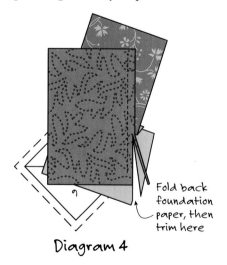

Fold back foundation paper, then trim here

Diagram 4

5. Add pieces 4, 5, and 6 in the same manner as piece 3, referring to Steps 3 and 4.

6. Repeat Steps 1 through 5 to make the second half of the block. Use a rotary cutter and ruler to trim the remaining edges of the block on the outer dashed lines, as shown in **Diagram 5.** Carefully remove the paper foundations.

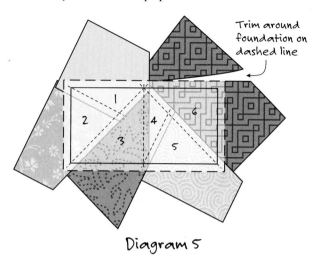

Trim around foundation on dashed line

Diagram 5

7. With right sides of the fabric together, pin and sew the two halves of the block together.

8. Repeat Steps 1 through 7 to make nine blocks total—one A, four B, and four C blocks.

ASSEMBLING THE QUILT

1. Referring to the **Assembly Diagram,** lay out the completed blocks in three rows of three blocks each. The top and bottom rows contain a B block, C block, and a B block. The middle row contains a C block, an A block, and a C block.

Assembly Diagram

2. With right sides together, sew the blocks together in horizontal rows. Press seams in opposite directions from row to row.

3. With right sides together, sew the rows of blocks together, matching seams carefully. Press the seam allowances toward the bottom of the quilt.

ADDING THE BORDERS

1. Sew the inner border to the outer border. Press the seams toward the outer border. Repeat to make four borders.

2. Read "Mitered Borders" on pages 248–249. Make the 45 degree angle cuts and mark the ¼-inch seam intersections as directed. Repeat for all four borders. Find the center of each border by folding it in half and marking the midpoint with a pin. Find the center of each quilt side by folding and marking with a pin. With right sides together, pin each border to the quilt, beginning at the center. Pin at each ¼-inch seam intersection, then generously pin the remaining areas, easing in any fullness. Sew each border to the quilt, stopping and starting at the marked ¼-inch seam intersections.

3. Miter the corners; see page 249 for details.

QUILTING AND FINISHING

1. Mark quilting designs as desired. The blocks in this quilt were handquilted ¼ inch inside the blue patches. The star points were left unquilted. A double chain was quilted in the outer border.

2. Cut a 25-inch square of backing fabric.

3. Layer the quilt top, batting, and backing, and baste the layers together. Quilt as desired.

4. Make double-fold binding and sew it to the quilt, following the directions on page 250.

Happy Endings

Once your quilt is complete, be sure to record your name and date of completion on the quilt or on a fabric label. For fun, use a leftover block from the quilt, sign your name and date, then slipstitch the block to the lower edge of the backing. Use fine-point permanent pens to add a verse, fancy scrollwork, or decorative motifs to a muslin or fabric label, then slipstitch it in place. If the quilt is a gift, note the recipient's name and the occasion. In later years, this label will serve as historical documentation of your talents, especially if the quilt will be passed from generation to generation.

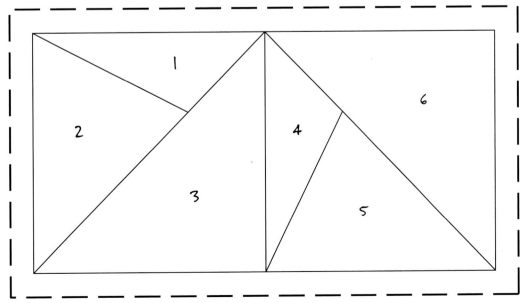

Block Pattern

Bed Topper

Finished Quilt Size: 63" square   **Finished Block Size: 7"**   **Number of Blocks: 49**

MATERIALS

4 yards assorted very dark blue prints

2 yards assorted medium dark blue prints

1 yard assorted medium blue prints

1½ yards light blue print

1⅜ yards red-orange print

½ yard light red-orange print

1 yard yellow-orange print

3¾ yards backing fabric

⅝ yard binding fabric

67-inch square of quilt batting

C U T T I N G

		First Cut		
FABRIC	**Used For**	**Shape**	**Dimensions**	**No. to Cut**
Assorted very dark blue prints	Star blocks	▬	6¼" × 3¾"	196
Assorted medium dark blue prints	Star blocks	▬	3½" × 5"	132
Assorted medium blue prints	Star blocks	▬	3½" × 5"	64

		First Cut		Second Cut		
FABRIC	**Used For**	**Strip Width**	**No. to Cut**	**Shape**	**Dimensions**	**No. to Cut**
Light blue print	Outer border	6½"	7*	—	—	—
Red-orange print	Star blocks	4½"	9	▬	4½" × 2¾"	116
Light red-orange print	Inner border	1½"	7*	—	—	—
Yellow-orange print	Star blocks	4½"	6	▭	4½" × 2¾"	80
Binding fabric	Binding	2½"	7	—	—	—

*Piece these together to create four 68-inch borders.

DIRECTIONS

1. Read the Star Dance project for color and fabric information, basic directions, and helpful tips. Using the **Bed Topper Block Pattern** on page 236, prepare 98 paper foundations.

2. Follow the directions in "Piecing the Blocks" on page 231 to make 49 blocks. Make 9 A blocks, 4 B blocks, 12 C blocks, and 24 D blocks; see the **Bed Topper Block Diagrams** and **Fabric Key** for fabric placement.

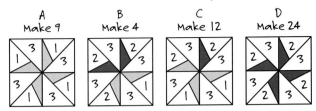

Bed Topper Block Diagrams

FABRIC KEY

1 Medium blue prints
2 Medium dark blue prints
3 Very dark blue prints

3. Lay out the blocks in seven rows of seven blocks each, referring to the **Bed Topper Quilt Diagram** for block placement.

4. Follow the directions in "Assembling the Quilt" and "Adding the Borders" on pages 232–233 to assemble the quilt top, piecing the border strips as necessary.

5. For the backing, cut the backing fabric in half crosswise, and trim the selvages. Cut 34-inch-wide segments from each piece, then sew the segments together, as shown in the **Backing Diagram.** Press the seams open. Position the backing with the seam in either the vertical or horizontal position.

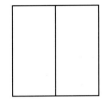

Backing Diagram

6. Layer the quilt top, batting, and backing, and baste the layers together. Quilt as desired.

7. Make double-fold binding and sew it to the quilt, following the directions on page 250.

Bed Topper Quilt Diagram

235

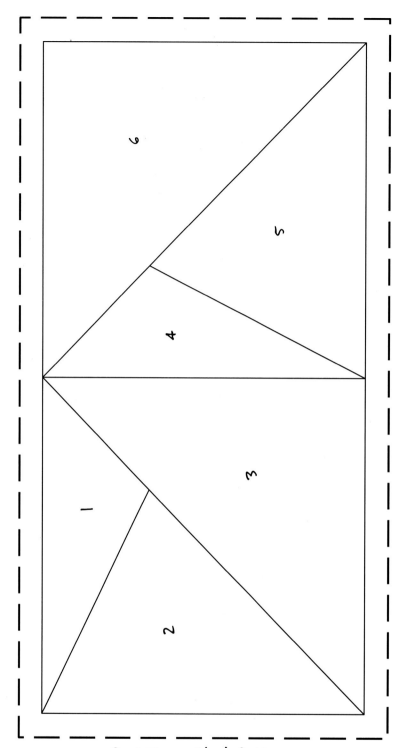

Bed Topper Block Pattern

Amethyst and Jade

This dazzling wall quilt, shown on page 238, features the rich, deep hues found in nature's most impressive gemstones. The blue and violet color families create a showcase of brilliant jewels that sparkle even more when topazlike yellow-orange and lustered ivory are added. Using Five Side-by-Side Colors with an Accent is an easy way to incorporate your new discoveries about color wheel relationships—since the colors are so similar, there's simply no room for error.

Harmony Featured

Five Side-by-Side Colors with an Accent

Colors Used

Blue-green, blue, blue-violet, violet, red-violet, accent of yellow-orange

MATERIALS

2½ yards medium and dark blue-green, blue, blue-violet, violet, and red-violet prints

¼ yard medium yellow-orange print

¾ yard medium black print

⅞ yard black print

½ yard ivory print

1 yard backing fabric

⅜ yard binding fabric

32-inch square of quilt batting

SKILL LEVEL: EASY

Finished Quilt Size: 28" square

Finished Block Size: 4"

Number of Blocks: 49

Magical Beginnings

Study the kaleidoscope blocks in this quilt. Each of the many fabrics is arranged in a pattern—in pairs or in sets of fours. Follow the color placement suggestions to give a sense of order to these colors, since they are so close on the color wheel.

The blocks in this quilt are paper pieced, so you will need to prepare paper foundations You'll find the foundation patterns on pages 244–245. Use the **Block Diagrams** on page 240 to determine which foundations to use for each block. You will need 34 A foundations, 16 B foundations, 40 C foundations, 4 D foundations, and 4 E foundations. For information on paper piecing, see page 248.

All seam allowances are ¼ inch unless specified otherwise.

CUTTING

Refer to the chart and cut the required number of strips and pieces. In some instances, you will cut rectangles instead of strips for a scrappier look.

C U T T I N G

FABRIC	Used For	First Cut Shape	First Cut Dimensions	First Cut No. to Cut	Second Cut Shape	Total No. Needed
Medium blue-green, blue, blue-violet, violet, and red-violet prints	Blocks 1, 2, 3, 4, 6, and 7	▬	2¾" × 4"	116	—	—
	Blocks 1 and 2	▪	3" × 3"	10	◪	20
Dark blue-green, blue, blue-violet, violet, and red-violet prints	Blocks 1, 2, 3, 4, and 5	▬	2¾" × 4"	100	—	—
	Block 4	■	3" × 3"	8	◪	16

FABRIC	Used For	First Cut Strip Width	First Cut No. to Cut	Second Cut Shape	Second Cut Dimensions	Second Cut No. to Cut	Third Cut Shape	Total No. Needed
Yellow-orange print	Blocks 1, 2, and 3	3"	2	▢	3" × 3"	16	◪	32
Medium black print	Block 6	3½"	3	▬	2½" × 5¼"	20	—	—
	Block 7	2¾"	1	▬	2¾" × 4"	4	—	—
Black print	Block 6	3"	5	▬	3" × 5"	25	—	—
	Block 7	2¾"	1	▬	2¾" × 5"	4	—	—
	Block 7 (E)	4¼"	1	▬	4¼" × 5¼"	4	—	—
Ivory print	Blocks 4 and 5	2¾"	3	▭	2¾" × 4"	32	—	—
Binding fabric	Binding	2½"	4	—	—	—	—	—

The cut sizes of the strips include generous seam allowances. You may wish to decrease the width of the strips in 1/8-inch increments as you become more familiar with paper piecing. Cut all strips across the crosswise grain, or fabric width. **Note:** Cut and piece one sample block before cutting all the fabric for the quilt.

PIECING THE BLOCKS

These instructions direct you in piecing one of the seven foundation blocks used for this quilt. As you piece each block, refer to the **Block Diagrams** and **Fabric Key** for the medium and dark fabric position, color placement, and foundation usage, since these factors differ in each of

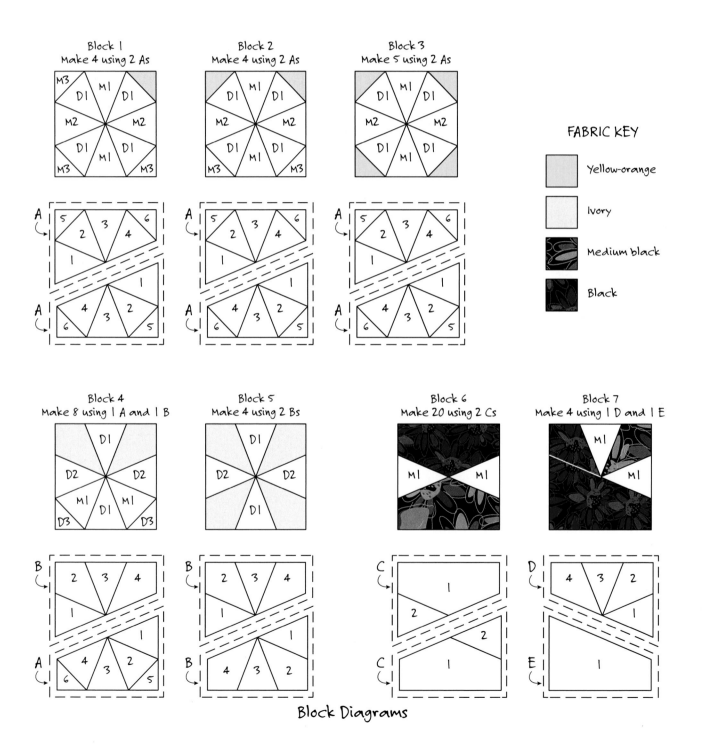

Block Diagrams

the seven blocks. The diagram labels include medium and dark fabric guidelines, such as D1 for dark fabric #1, D2 for dark fabric #2, and M1 for medium fabric #1.

This quilt is scrappy, so use a variety of mediums and darks, paying particular attention to the number of times a fabric is used within one block. Even though you need to make Block 1 four times, be sure each Block 1 uses different colors and fabrics. The diagrams include areas of color that remain constant in a block, such as yellow-orange or ivory. Blocks 1 through 5 contain two or three elements: kaleidoscopes, background, and sometimes corner triangles. Blocks 6 and 7 contain three elements: inner "border" pieces, triangles, and outer "border" pieces.

1. Fabric pieces are positioned on the back, or un-marked, side of the foundation. Pieces are added in numerical order starting at 1. All sewing takes place on the front side of the foundation, directly on the drawn lines. All lines on the foundation, ex-cept the dashed one around the outer perimeter, are seam lines. To begin, layer a background piece on top of a kaleidoscope piece with right sides to-gether. Position these pieces underneath one of the foundations, so that the background piece lies against the foundation; see **Diagram 1.** The edges of the piece must extend ¼ inch beyond the seam line between 1 and 2. Making 12 to 14 stitches per inch, sew on the line separating 1 and 2, beginning and ending the stitching approximately ¼ inch on either side of the line.

2. Flip the kaleidoscope piece into a right-side-up position, pressing it firmly in place, as shown in **Diagram 2.** Hold the foundation up to the light with the paper side toward you. You will now be able to see the shadow created by the kaleidoscope fabric. The shadow should overlap all lines drawn for the kaleidoscope piece, and the overlap should be sufficient to create a stable seam allowance. If it is not, use a seam ripper to remove the kaleido-scope piece from the foundation, then reposition the piece and try again. This ensures that there will be enough seam allowance on all sides when you add the adjacent fabric pieces.

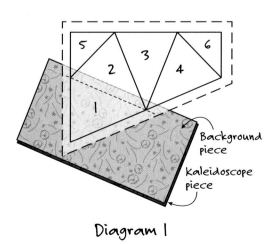

Background piece

Kaleidoscope piece

Diagram 1

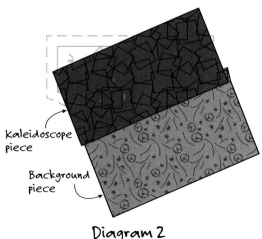

Kaleidoscope piece

Background piece

Diagram 2

3. Referring to **Diagram 3,** place a background piece right sides together with the 1 and 2 pieces. Pin the loose edges of pieces 1 and 2 to the foundation to avoid lumps when adding the next piece. Be sure the new background piece extends at least ¼ inch beyond the seam line between 2 and 3, then sew along this seam line.

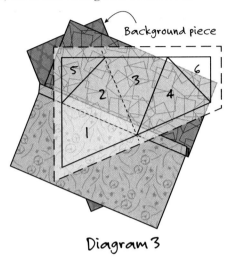

Diagram 3

4. Trim the background and kaleidoscope pieces to a scant ¼ inch beyond the seam line between 2 and 3, as shown in **Diagram 4;** be sure to fold the foundation paper away from the fabric to avoid cutting it as you trim the seam allowance. Flip the background piece into a right-side-up position, pressing it firmly in place.

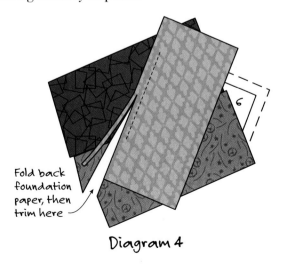

Diagram 4

5. Add the next kaleidoscope piece in the same manner as the background piece in Steps 3 and 4.

6. To make it easier to align the corner triangles (pieces 5 and 6), use a rotary cutter and ruler to trim around the block to remove excess fabric before adding the corners. Be sure to trim on the dashed line, not the solid line, of the foundation, as shown in **Diagram 5.** Take care not to trim away the actual dashed line.

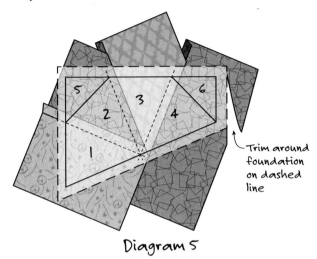

Diagram 5

7. If the block has corner triangles, place a corner triangle right sides together with the kaleidoscope piece, and sew the seam line between 2 and 5, as shown in **Diagram 6.** Trim the seam, flip the corner triangle into a right-side-up position, and press. Add the remaining corner in the same manner. Trim the excess fabric from both corners. Carefully remove the paper foundation.

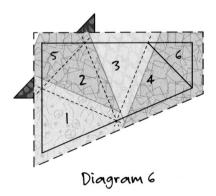

Diagram 6

8. Repeat Steps 1 through 7 to make the second half of the block, using the appropriate foundation and fabric color as indicated in the **Block Diagrams** and **Fabric Key** on page 240.

With right sides of the fabric together, pin and sew the two halves of the block together, being sure to match any center points, as shown in **Diagram 7.**

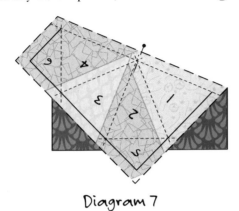

Diagram 7

9. Using the **Block Diagrams** and **Fabric Key** and foundations A, B, C, or D, paper piece the remaining blocks for the quilt. For foundation E, place the wrong side of the fabric against the paper foundation. Baste the fabric to the foundation within the ¼-inch seam allowance area to hold the fabric in place. Join foundations D and E together to form a block in the same manner as the other blocks.

ASSEMBLING THE QUILT

1. Referring to the **Block Chart,** lay out the completed blocks in seven rows of seven blocks each, matching the block number to the number on the chart. Be sure the yellow-orange and ivory fabrics in the blocks are placed correctly to create the five light circles, as shown in the **Assembly Diagram.**

7	6	6	6	6	6	7
6	1	4	2	4	1	6
6	4	3	5	3	4	6
6	2	5	3	5	2	6
6	4	3	5	3	4	6
6	1	4	2	4	1	6
7	6	6	6	6	6	7

Block Chart

Assembly Diagram

2. With right sides together, sew the blocks together in horizontal rows. Press seams in opposite directions from row to row.

3. With right sides together, sew the rows of blocks together, matching seams carefully. Press the seam allowances toward the bottom edge of the quilt.

HINTS FROM HAZEL

Be careful not to tug or pull too hard on the foundation paper when removing it from the blocks, since you may distort your seam or stretch a bias edge. If there are stubborn bits of foundation paper caught under stitched seams, use a pair of tweezers or hemostats to gently remove them.

QUILTING AND FINISHING

1. Mark the quilt top for quilting. This quilt was quilted entirely along the seams so the fabrics would take center stage.

2. Cut a 32-inch square of backing fabric.

3. Layer the quilt top, batting, and backing, and baste the layers together. Quilt as desired.

4. Make double-fold binding and sew it to the quilt, following the directions on page 250.

Happy Endings

What a treat—once the blocks were assembled, you were finished with the quilt top! There weren't any borders to add, corners to miter, or seams to match, and that's a happy ending all by itself. Why not design a similar quilt that's complete when the last row of blocks is sewn together? The outer row of blocks could be a companion design to create an un-border. Then just layer with batting and a backing, tie it with pearl cotton knots, and enjoy!

Work a Little Color Magic

Making Your Quilts Sizzle

Wouldn't it be great if there were a single color that was guaranteed to give a quilt ZING? Well, such a magical color has not been discovered yet, but there are ways to use color to make your quilts sizzle. Oftentimes, the spark your quilt needs most is the addition of a lighter fabric than those you have been using. Even in a dark, moody quilt, the addition of a fabric that is noticeably lighter will liven up the entire design. A touch of a clear, bright color, especially in a darker quilt, provides the perfect sizzle. The opposite is true for a quilt that seems too light; adding darks will breathe new life into the quilt.

Another way to make a quilt "pop" is to add an unexpected color. The accent harmonies are built around this theory—an unusual color is a feast for the eyes!

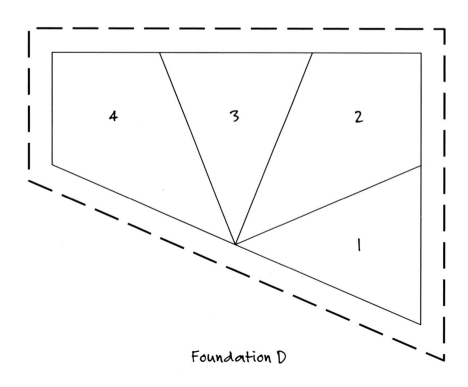

Foundation D

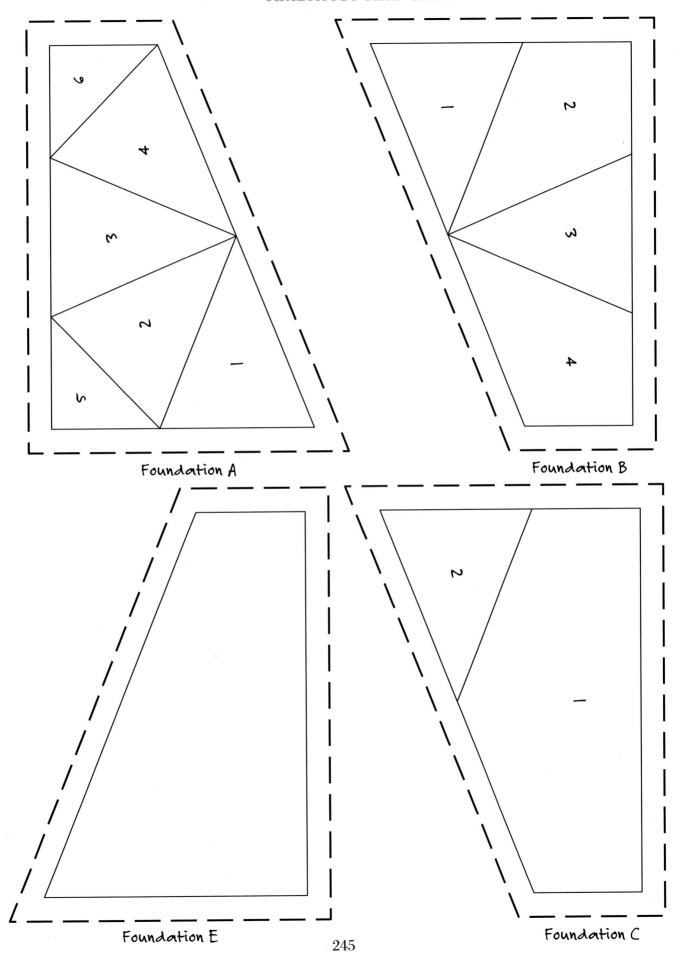

Foundation A

Foundation B

Foundation E

Foundation C

Quilts are sewn together with heartstrings

Back to Basics

Discover brief descriptions of basic techniques as well as
tips designed to make your quiltmaking successful and fun.
Refer to this information for a quick review of the quilting
process, or use it to hone your newly acquired skills.

ROTARY CUTTING

The cutting instructions in this book use quick rotary-cutting techniques whenever possible. When you use a rotary cutter, move the blade away from yourself, and always slide the blade guard into place as soon as you stop cutting.

1. Fold the fabric with the selvage edges together. Square up the end of the fabric; see **Diagram 1.** Place a ruled square on the fold, and slide a 6 × 24-inch ruler against the side of the square. Hold the ruler in place, remove the square, and cut along the edge of the ruler.

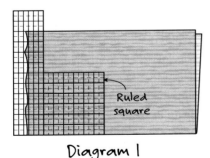

Diagram 1

2. Cut strips on the crosswise grain, then cut them into smaller pieces as the directions specify. **Diagram 2** shows a strip cut into squares. You can also cut rectangles. Find the strip width specified in the cutting directions, then locate the measurement on the ruler. Align that number's guideline on the ruler with the squared-up edge of

the fabric. The other edge of the ruler serves as the cutting guide; slide the rotary cutter along the edge of the ruler, cutting away from yourself.

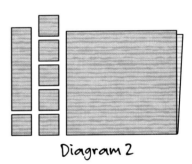

Diagram 2

3. Once a strip has been cut into squares, the squares can also be cut into two or four triangles by making diagonal cuts, as shown in **Diagram 3.**

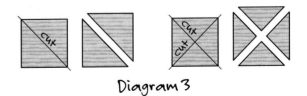

Diagram 3

TEMPLATES

Patterns in this book are printed full size. Lay template plastic over the page, trace the patterns onto the plastic with a permanent pen, and cut them out with scissors. Copy letters and arrows onto your templates. Draw around the template on the wrong side of the fabric; see **Diagram 4.** The outer solid line is the cutting line, and the inner dashed line is the sewing line.

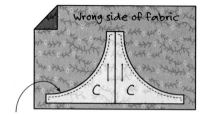

Tracing and cutting line includes seam allowance
Diagram 4

MACHINE PIECING

The standard quiltmaking seam allowance is ¼ inch. Machine sew a sample to check the accuracy of the seam allowance; adjust as needed. Set the stitch length for 10 stitches per inch. Place the fabric pieces right sides together, then sew from raw edge to raw edge.

PAPER PIECING

With paper piecing, an entire block is drawn to scale on tracing paper or a similar-weight paper foundation. The only seam allowance included is the one around the outer perimeter. The technique involves positioning the fabric on one side of the foundation (the reverse, or unmarked, side) and sewing on the opposite side (the front, marked side). Seams are stitched directly onto one of the marked lines. Since the fabric will be sewn to the back of the foundation, the finished block will always be a mirror image of the pattern.

There are several ways to transfer the block pattern onto your foundation. Use a hot-iron transfer pen to draw the full-size block onto the paper. The image can be ironed onto five or six foundations before the lines need to be redrawn. Use photocopies for smaller blocks, checking to make sure blocks are square and true to size. A light box can be used to trace a block directly onto the foundation. You will need a separate foundation for each whole block or section of a block.

The paper piecing instructions in this book contain recommended sizes for strip widths. The strip width is based on the finished size, plus seam allowances and a bit extra. When you paper piece, it's usually best to have larger-than-needed strips and pieces to give you more flexibility when positioning them.

Set a shorter-than-normal stitch length since smaller stitches are less likely to be distorted when foundations are pulled away.

PRESSING

Each project gives pressing instructions, but there are general guidelines you can follow. Press a seam to one side before joining it with another piece. Press seams toward darker fabrics. Press seams of adjacent rows of blocks, or rows within blocks, in opposite directions; see **Diagram 5.**

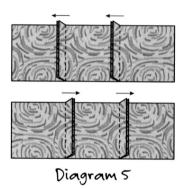

Diagram 5

MITERED BORDERS

If there are two or more borders to miter, sew them together and treat them as one unit, pressing seams toward the outside border. Taking measurements through the horizontal or vertical center of the quilt, cut the top and bottom borders 4 to 5 inches longer than the *finished* width of the quilt, and cut the side borders 4 to 5 inches longer than the *finished* length of the quilt.

Lay the border in position next to the quilt top, then cut one end of a border at a 45 degree angle; see **Diagram 6.** Measure the shorter edge of the border and mark the point that equals the width of the quilt minus ¼ inch. Using this mark as a guide, cut a 45 degree angle on this end of the border in the opposite direction from the other 45 degree cut.

Mark the quilt width measurement minus ¼", then cut this end at a 45 degree angle

45°   45°

Diagram 6

Matching ¼-inch seam intersections at the corners and on the short side of the border, sew the top border to the quilt, beginning and ending stitching at the ¼-inch marks; see **Diagram 7.** Backstitch. Repeat for the bottom and side borders.

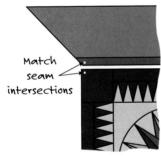

Match seam intersections

Diagram 7

Pin and sew all four mitered corners, beginning at the outside edge of the quilt and working inward toward the quilt top; see **Diagram 8.** Backstitch.

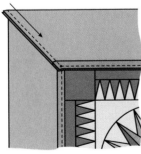

Diagram 8

QUILTING DESIGNS

Quilting suggestions are included with each project. Mark your quilting designs before layering your quilt. For light fabrics, use a 0.5 mm mechanical lead pencil. Place the pattern under the quilt top, and trace the quilting design directly onto the fabric, marking a very thin line. For dark fabrics, lay a quilting stencil on the right side of the fabric, then mark with a silver or white pencil or chalk marker.

LAYERING AND BASTING

To layer, fold the quilt backing in half lengthwise and press, to form a center line. Place the back, wrong side up, on the basting table. Fold the batting in half lengthwise and lay it on the quilt backing, aligning the center lines. Open out the batting, smoothing any wrinkles. Fold the quilt top in half lengthwise, right sides together, and lay it on the batting, aligning the fold with the center of the batting. Unfold the top and smooth it out.

If you are handquilting, use a long darning needle and white sewing thread to baste the layers together, making lines of basting 3 inches apart. Baste from the center out or make horizontal and vertical lines of basting in a lattice fashion. If you plan to machine quilt, use 1-inch safety pins to secure the layers together, pinning from the center out approximately every 3 inches.

HANDQUILTING

Use a hoop or frame to hold the quilt layers taut. Work with one hand on top of the quilt and the other hand underneath. Use short quilting needles, called betweens, in either size 9 or 10. To start, thread a needle with quilting thread and knot the end. Insert the needle through the quilt top and batting about 1 inch away from where you will begin stitching. Bring the needle to the surface to make the first stitch. Gently tug on the thread to pop the knot through the quilt top and bury it in the batting; see **Diagram 9.**

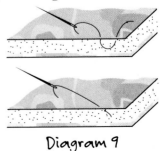

Diagram 9

To make quilting stitches, insert the needle through all quilt layers. When you feel the tip of the needle with your underneath finger, gently guide it back up through the quilt. When the needle comes through the top of the quilt, press your thimble on the end with the eye to guide it down again through the quilt layers. Continue to quilt in this manner, taking two or three small running stitches at a time. See **Diagram 10.**

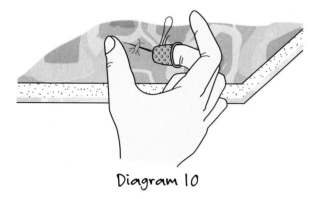

Diagram 10

To end stitching, bring the needle to the top of the quilt, just past the last stitch. Referring to **Diagram 11,** make a knot at the surface by bringing the needle under the thread where it comes out of the fabric and up through the loop of thread it creates. Repeat this knot and insert the needle into the hole where the thread comes out of the fabric. Run the needle inside the batting for an inch and bring it back to the surface. Tug gently on the thread to pop the knot through the quilt top and into the batting layer. Clip the thread.

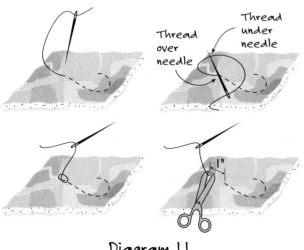

Thread over needle

Thread under needle

Diagram 11

MACHINE QUILTING

To secure the thread at the beginning and end of a machine quilting design, adjust the stitch length on your machine to make several very short stitches. For machine-guided quilting, use a walking foot for quilting straight lines. Keep the feed dogs up and move all three layers as smoothly as you can under the needle. Machine-guided quilting is ideal for quilting in the ditch and creating grids.

For free-motion quilting, use a darning or machine embroidery foot and disengage the sewing machine feed dogs. For best results, choose continuous-line quilting designs so you won't have to begin and end threads frequently. Guide the marked design under the needle with both hands, working at a steady pace.

BINDING

Double-fold binding can be made from either straight-grain or bias strips. To make binding, cut strips in the desired width. Place the strips right sides together so that each strip is set ¼ inch in from the end of the other strip; see **Diagram 12.** Sew a diagonal seam and trim, leaving a ¼-inch seam allowance. Press the seam open. Fold the strip in half lengthwise, wrong sides together, and press. Pin raw edges of the binding together and sew ¼ inch from the raw edges.

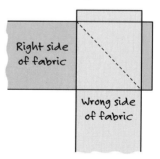

Right side of fabric

Wrong side of fabric

Diagram 12

To attach the binding, trim the batting and backing even with the quilt top. Beginning in the middle of a side, place the strip right sides together with the quilt top. Align the raw edges, and make a 45 degree angle fold at the beginning of the binding; see **Diagram 13.** Pin the binding.

Sew the binding around the perimeter of the quilt, using a ⅜-inch seam. Sew through all layers of the quilt.

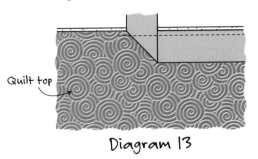

Diagram 13

As you approach a corner of the quilt, stop stitching ⅜ inch from the raw edge of the corner. Backstitch two or three stitches and remove the quilt from the machine. Fold the binding strip up at a 45 degree angle, as shown in **Diagram 14.** Fold the strip back down so there is a fold at the upper edge, as shown in the diagram. Begin sewing at the top edge of the quilt, continuing to the next corner. Miter all four corners in this same manner.

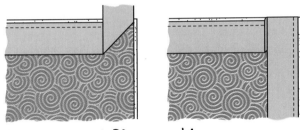

Diagram 14

To finish the binding seam, place the ending section over the angled beginning section. Sew through all layers, as shown in **Diagram 15.** Trim all edges.

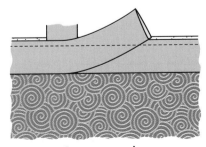

Diagram 15

Note: If you plan to add a hanging sleeve, follow the Hanging Sleeve directions to make and attach the sleeve before finishing the binding.

Hand sew the joining closed. Turn the binding to the back of the quilt and hand sew the folded edge in place, covering the machine stitches with the folded edge; see **Diagram 16.** Fold the adjacent sides on the back and take several stitches in the miter. Add several stitches to the miters on the front to secure them in place.

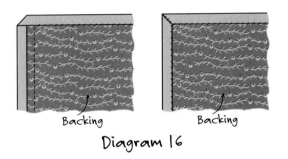

Diagram 16

HANGING SLEEVE

If you plan to hang your quilt on a wall or display it at a quilt show, you may want to add a hanging sleeve to the back to evenly distribute the weight of the quilt. Cut a strip of muslin or matching backing fabric that measures 8½ inches × the width of the finished quilt minus 1 inch. Machine hem the short ends of the strip by turning under ½ inch on each end and pressing; then turn under another ½ inch and sew next to the fold.

Fold and press the strip in half lengthwise, wrong sides together, aligning the two long raw edges. Position the raw edges of the sleeve so they align with the top raw edges on the back of the quilt. The binding should already be sewn on the front but not turned to the back of the quilt. Pin the sleeve in place.

Machine sew the sleeve to the back of the quilt, sewing on the right side of the quilt on top of the stitches that hold the binding. Turn the binding to the back of the quilt and hand sew the binding in place so that the binding covers the raw edge of the sleeve. You may need to trim away more batting and backing on top of the quilt in order to turn the binding easily. Hand sew the bottom loose edge of the sleeve in place.

ABOUT THE AUTHORS

ann Seely and Joyce Stewart are sisters and were born and raised in central Utah. Both of them attended Brigham Young University and met their husbands while attending the university. Ann and her husband, Richard, have 3 children and 1 grandchild. They live in Salt Lake City, Utah. Joyce and her husband, Lynn, live in Rexburg, Idaho, and have 5 children and 11 grandchildren.

They began quilting in 1983 when they strip pieced a Lone Star quilt for a niece's wedding. With just one quilt, they were hooked! But with several hundred miles separating them, additional joint projects proved difficult. So Ann and Joyce each pursued quiltmaking separately, often competing against each other in local quilt shows, but always sharing the joy of each other's successes. Their quilts have won awards in many national contests, including the Hoffman Quilt Challenge, the American Quilter's Society show, the Lands' End and *Good Housekeeping* All-American Quilt Contest, and the Museum of American Folk Art's Great American Quilt Contest. Their work has been prominently featured in magazines and books, such as *Quilter's Newsletter Magazine*, *McCall's Quilting*, *American Quilter*, *America's Best Quilting Projects*, and *Quick and Easy Scrap Quilts*.

In 1992, they co-authored the book *Sisters and Quilts: Threads That Bind*. Soon they began teaching at quilt guilds and shows across the country, including the American Quilter's Society show in Paducah, and have discovered that their class, "Color Magic for Quilters," is always a big hit!

ACKNOWLEDGMENTS

With love to our parents, Allen and Ava Winterton, without whom the color memories would not be possible.

Ann would like to thank her family for their support and encouragement: Richard; Michael and Jennifer Seely and Richard; David; and Steven.

Joyce would like to thank her family: Lynn; Ron and Susan Watkins and Trevor, Tyson, Shari, and Staci; Greg and Lisa Stewart and Brandon, Ryan, Jason, and Analisa; Jim and Shari Shirley and Scot, Robert, and Jameson; Steven; and Allen.

Special thanks to Harold and Dorthey Chase for allowing photographs to be taken at their quilt shop, Quilt, Quilt, Quilt, etc., in Sandy, Utah.

We would also like to acknowledge quiltmakers everywhere. We believe that a quiltmaker is more than just someone who makes quilts. A quiltmaker loves geometric shapes, the soft curves of floral appliqué, the interplay of color, freshly pressed fabric, and the feel of quilting stitches. Quiltmaker is a term of endearment!

Quilts designed, pieced, and quilted by Ann Seely:

Butterflies Are Free	Mystic Garden
Charmed Memories	Night Crystals
Five Baskets	Romantica
Hazel's Scrappy	Rosewood
Sampler	Sailboats
Mardi Gras	When Stars Collide

Quilts designed and pieced by Joyce Stewart, and quilted by Ann Seely:

Amethyst and Jade	Star Bright
Flight of Fancy	Star Dance
Garden Maze	Windmills and
Pathways	Daisies

Quilts designed, pieced, and quilted by Joyce Stewart:

Autumn Glow	SpinWheels
Northern Lights	Tribute to Mother
Seascape	Welcome

RECOMMENDED READING

Beyer, Jinny. *The Quilter's Album of Blocks and Borders*. McLean, VA: EPM Publications, 1986.

Blake, Wendon. *The Color Book*. New York: Watson-Guptill Publications, 1981.

Branley, Franklin M. *Color, From Rainbows to Lasers*. New York: Thomas Y. Crowell Company, 1978.

Dunn, Charles. *Conversations in Paint: A Notebook of Fundamentals*. New York: Workman Publishing Company, 1995.

Garau, Augusto. *Color Harmonies*. Translated by Nicola Bruno. Chicago: University of Chicago Press, 1993.

Gatto, Joseph A. *Elements of Design: Color and Value*. Worcester, MA: Davis Publications, Inc., 1974.

Gerritsen, Frans. *Theory and Practice of Color*. New York: Van Nostrand Reinhold. 1975.

Goldberg, Rhoda O. *The New Quilting and Patchwork Dictionary*. New York: Crown Publishing Group, 1988.

Itten, Johannes. *The Art of Color*. New York: Van Nostrand Reinhold, 1973.

———. *Elements of Color*. New York: Van Nostrand Reinhold, 1970.

Leland, Nita. *Exploring Color*. Cincinnati, OH: North Light Books, 1991.

Magaret, Pat M., and Donna Slusser. *Watercolor Quilts*. Bothell, WA: That Patchwork Place, 1993.

Mathieson, Judy. *Mariner's Compass: An American Quilt Classic*. Martinez, CA: C&T Publishing, 1986.

McClun, Diana, and Laura Nownes. *Quilts! Quilts!! Quilts!!! The Complete Guide to Quiltmaking*. Lincolnwood, IL: The Quilt Digest Press, 1989.

McKelvey, Susan. *Color for Quilters*. Vol II. Millersville, MD: Wallflower Designs, 1994.

———. *Creative Ideas for Color and Fabric*. (The Classic American Quilt Collection Series.) Emmaus, PA: Rodale Press, 1996.

Penders, Mary Coyne. *Color and Cloth: The Quiltmaker's Ultimate Handbook*. Lincolnwood, IL: The Quilt Digest Press, 1989.

Stockton, James. *Designer's Guide to Color: Over One Thousand Color Combinations*. San Francisco: Chronicle Books, 1984.

Van Wyk, Helen. *Color Mixing the Van Wyk Way*. Cincinnati, OH: North Light Books, 1995.

Wells, Jean. *Patchwork Quilts Made Easy*. Emmaus, PA: Rodale Press, 1994.

Color a Quilt

Colors evoke many thoughts from the heart,
Inspired in us all by creations of art.
As varied in shade as the hues of a quilt
Are countless designs waiting still to be built.

The colors of warmth—comfy, cozy, and bright,
The colors that glow like a fire at night,
The colors of cool—icy purple and gray,
The colors that melt in the hot light of day.

The colors that run gently, rippling true,
The colors that contrast, as orange and blue,
The colors that clash and clamor and ring,
The colors that sigh and whisper and sing.

So color a quilt—let the colors ring true,
And the colors will bring inspiration to you
And to others who soon will be touched by your art,
For colors send messages straight to the heart.

Shari Jo Shirley
daughter of Joyce Stewart

Index

A

Accent
  choosing, 16, 244
  Colors on a Triangle with, 112–14,
    216, 217
  Five Side-by-Side Colors with,
    42–45, 237, 238
  Opposite Colors with, 52–54, 139,
    141, 144, 145
  Three Alternating Colors with,
    100–103, 186, 187
  Three Side-by-Side Colors with,
    34–37
  Two Colors Separated by Two
    Colors with, 84–87
Amethyst and Jade, 42, 43, 237–45
Analogous colors, 31
Analogous with an accent, 35
Autumn Glow, 112, 113, 216–27

B

Basting, 249
Beads, 150, 183
Binding, 250–51
Black, 25, 26, 49
Block makeovers, 140–41
Blue, 137, 138, 139, 141
  in Amethyst and Jade, 42, 43,
    237, 238
  in Five Baskets, 96, 97
  mood evoked by, 130
  in Night Crystals, 104, 105, 205,
    206
  in opposite color schemes, 49
  in Sailboats, 100, 101, 186, 187
  in Seascape, 30, 31, 175, 176
  in Star Dance, 68, 69, 228, 229,
    230
  symbolism of, 15
  in Welcome, 92, 93
  in When Stars Collide, 60, 61,
    158, 159
  in Windmills and Daisies, 24, 25,
    166, 167
Blue-green, 138, 141
  in Amethyst and Jade, 42, 43,
    237, 238

  in Autumn Glow, 112, 113,
    216, 217
  in Charmed Memories, 84, 85
  in Hazel's Scrappy Sampler, 72, 73
  in Mardi Gras, 108, 109
  in Seascape, 30, 31, 175, 176
Blue-violet, 140, 141
  in Amethyst and Jade, 42, 43,
    237, 238
  in Butterflies Are Free, 52, 53,
    144, 145
  in Mystic Garden, 48, 49
  in Northern Lights, 38, 39
  in When Stars Collide, 60, 61,
    158, 159
Borders, mitered, 248–49
Butterflies Are Free, 52, 53, 144–50

C

Charmed Memories, 84, 85
Colors on a Triangle, 108–10
Colors on a Triangle with an Accent,
  112–14, 216, 217
Color wheel, 12–14, 16, 17–19
Complementary colors, 49
Contrast, 25, 141
Cool colors
  for accents, 54
  mood created by, 71
  in One Color harmony, 25
  in opposite color schemes, 49, 54
  in Three Alternating Colors har-
    mony, 97
  in Two Colors Separated by Four
    Colors harmony, 93
  in Two Colors Separated by Three
    Colors harmony, 89
Cream, 25, 49, 105

D

Darks, 132, 133, 154, 214
Designs, quilting, 249
Dye(s)
  artificial, 114
  bleeding of, 202
  fixative, 67
  primary colors in, 12, 13

E

Every Other Color, 104–6, 137, 139,
  205, 206
Extended analogous color harmony, 39
Extended analogous with an accent, 43

F

Fading, 196
Five Baskets, 96, 97
Five Side-by-Side Colors, 38–41
Five Side-by-Side Colors with an
  Accent, 42–45, 237, 238
Flight of Fancy, 56, 57
Folding a quilt, 196
Four Points on a Square, 72–74

G

Garden Maze, 116, 117, 212–15
Gray, 25, 26, 52, 53, 98, 161
Green, 137, 138, 139, 140, 141
  in Flight of Fancy, 56, 57
  in Main Color with Three Opposite
    Colors harmony, 65
  mood evoked by, 127
  in Night Crystals, 104, 105,
    205, 206
  in opposite color schemes, 49, 50
  in Pathways, 198, 199
  in Romantica, 64, 65
  in Sailboats, 100, 101, 186, 187
  in Seascape, 30, 31, 175, 176
  symbolism of, 15
  in Tribute to Mother, 34, 35

H

Handquilting, 249–50
Hanging sleeve, 251
Harmonies
  Multicolor (see Multicolor har-
    monies)
  Opposite Color (see Opposite
    colors)
  overview of, 16–17

Side-by-Side Color (*see* Side-by-side colors)
Single Color (*see* Single Color harmonies)
Spaced Color (*see* Spaced Color harmonies)
Triangle Color (*see* Triangle Color harmonies)
Hazel's Scrappy Sampler, 72, 73

L

Labels, 233
Large-scale prints, 110, 134, 150
Layering, 249
Lights, 132, 133, 154, 214

M

Machine piecing, 248
Machine quilting, 204, 250
Main Color with Many Colors, 120–23, 136, 198, 199
Main Color with Three Opposite Colors, 64–67
Makeovers, block, 140–41
Many Colors, 116–18, 138, 212, 213
Mardi Gras, 108, 109
Marking quilts, 156, 201, 249
Mediums, 132, 133, 214
Medium-scale prints, 140
Mitered borders, 248–49
Monochromatic, definition of, 25
Mood, 91, 126–131, 139, 141
Multicolor fabrics, 138
Multicolor harmonies
  Main Color with Many Colors, 120–23, 136, 198, 199
  Many Colors, 116–18, 138, 212, 213
Mystic Garden, 48, 49

N

Neutral(s)
  backgrounds, 26, 98, 105
  in Butterflies Are Free, 53
  with complementary colors, 49
  in Flight of Fancy, 57
  gray thread, 161
  in One Color harmony, 25
  in Two Colors Separated by Three Colors harmony, 89

in Welcome, 92, 93
Night Crystals, 104, 105, 205–11
Northern Lights, 38, 39, 40

O

One Color harmony, 24–27, 166–67
Opposite colors, 48–50, 137
  Opposite Color harmonies
    Four Points on a Square, 72–74
    Main Color with Three Opposite Colors, 64–67
    Opposite Colors with an Accent, 52–54, 139, 141, 144, 145
    Splitting the Opposite, 68–71, 228, 229
    Three Colors and Their Opposites, 60–62, 158, 159
    Two Colors and Their Opposites, 56–58, 137, 138, 139, 140
Opposite Colors with an Accent, 52–54, 139, 141, 144, 145
Orange, 39, 137, 138, 139, 141
  in Charmed Memories, 84, 85
  mood evoked by, 131
  in Night Crystals, 104, 105, 205, 206
  in opposite color schemes, 49
  in Sailboats, 100, 101, 186, 187
  symbolism of, 15
  in Tribute to Mother, 34, 35
  in When Stars Collide, 60, 61, 158, 159

P

Paper foundation piecing, 239, 240–43, 248
Pathways, 198–204
Polychromatic, definition of, 117
Pressing, 248
Prewashing fabrics, 67, 150, 202
Primary colors, 12–14
Print(s)
  in blocks, 83, 86
  conversational, 102
  fabric, cutting, 44
  how to correct problems with, 140–41
  large-scale, 110, 134, 150
  medium-scale, 140
  mixing, 83, 86

selecting, 134
small-scale, 140
Prism, 13
Pure colors, 12

Q

Quilting designs, 249

R

Red, 136, 137, 138, 139, 140, 141
  in Five Baskets, 96, 97
  in Flight of Fancy, 56, 57
  in Main Color with Three Opposite Colors harmony, 65
  mood evoked by, 126
  in Night Crystals, 104, 105, 205, 206
  in Northern Lights, 38, 39
  in opposite color schemes, 49, 50
  in Rosewood, 80, 81
  symbolism of, 15
  in Tribute to Mother, 34, 35
Red-orange, 136, 138
  in Butterflies Are Free, 52, 53, 144, 145
  in Hazel's Scrappy Sampler, 72, 73
  in Northern Lights, 38, 39
  in Star Dance, 68, 69, 228, 229
  in Tribute to Mother, 35, 334
  in Welcome, 92, 93
Red-violet, 136, 140
  in Amethyst and Jade, 42, 43, 237, 238
  in Autumn Glow, 112, 113, 216, 217
  in Charmed Memories, 84, 85
  in Mardi Gras, 108, 109
  in Northern Lights, 38, 39
  in Romantica, 64, 65
  in Star Bright, 88, 89
Romantica, 64, 65
Rosewood, 80, 81
Rotary cutting, 231, 247

S

Sailboats, 100, 101, 186–97
Scale, in one-color quilts, 25
Seascape, 30, 31, 175–85
Secondary colors, 13, 14
Shade, 13, 49

Side-by-side colors
  Side-by-Side Color harmonies
    Five Side-by-Side Colors, 38–41
    Five Side-by-Side Colors with an Accent, 42–45, 237, 238
    Three Side-by-Side Colors, 30–33, 136, 138, 141, 175, 176
    Three Side-by-Side Colors with an Accent, 34–37
Single Color harmonies, 23–27, 166, 167
Small-scale prints, 140
Solids, 83, 134, 200
Sorting fabrics, 223
Spaced Color harmonies
  Every Other Color, 104–6, 137, 139, 205, 206
  Three Alternating Colors, 96–99, 138
  Three Alternating Colors with an Accent, 100–103, 186, 187
  Two Colors Separated by Four Colors, 92–95
  Two Colors Separated by One Color, 76–79, 138, 140, 151, 152
  Two Colors Separated by Three Colors, 88–91, 138, 139, 141
  Two Colors Separated by Two Colors, 80–83
  Two Colors Separated by Two Colors with an Accent, 84–87
SpinWheels, 76, 77, 151–57
Splitting the Opposite, 68–71, 228, 229
Star Bright, 88, 89
Star Dance, 68, 69, 228–36
Storage ideas, 150, 196
Symbolism of colors, 15

Templates, 147, 247–48
Tertiary colors, 14
Tetrad, 73
Texture, visual, 136–37, 177
Thread, 161, 163, 204
Three Alternating Colors, 96–99, 138
Three Alternating Colors with an Accent, 100–103, 186, 187
Three Colors and Their Opposites, 60–62, 158, 159
Three Side-by-Side Colors, 30–33, 136, 138, 141, 175, 176
Three Side-by-Side Colors with an Accent, 34–37
Tint, 13, 49
Tone, 13
Triad, 109
Triangle Color harmonies
  Colors on a Triangle, 108–10
  Colors on a Triangle with an Accent, 112–14, 216, 217
Tribute to Mother, 34, 35
Triple complementary, 61
Two Colors and Their Opposites, 56–58, 137, 138, 139, 140
Two Colors Separated by Four Colors, 92–95
Two Colors Separated by One Color, 76–79, 138, 140, 151, 152
Two Colors Separated by Three Colors, 88–91, 138, 139, 141
Two Colors Separated by Two Colors, 80–83
Two Colors Separated by Two Colors with an Accent, 84–87

Value, 13, 50, 106, 132, 133, 214
Violet, 39, 137, 138, 139
  in Amethyst and Jade, 42, 43, 237, 238
  in Five Baskets, 96, 97
  in Flight of Fancy, 56, 57
  in Hazel's Scrappy Sampler, 72, 73
  mood evoked by, 128
  in Night Crystals, 104, 105, 205, 206
  in Northern Lights, 38, 39
  in opposite color schemes, 49, 137
  in Sailboats, 100, 101, 186, 187
  symbolism of, 15
  in When Stars Collide, 60, 61, 158, 159
Visual texture, 136–37, 177

Warm colors
  for accents, 54
  in Five Side-by-Side Colors, 39
  mood created by, 71

in One Color harmony, 25
in opposite color schemes, 49, 54
in Three Alternating Colors harmony, 97
in Two Colors Separated by Four Colors harmony, 93
in Two Colors Separated by Three Colors harmony, 89
Welcome, 92, 93
When Stars Collide, 60, 61, 158–65
White, 25, 26, 49, 98, 105
Windmills and Daisies, 24, 25, 166–74

Yellow, 137, 138, 139
  in Flight of Fancy, 56, 57
  in Hazel's Scrappy Sampler, 72, 73
  mood evoked by, 129
  in Night Crystals, 104, 105, 205, 206
  in opposite color schemes, 49, 137
  in Romantica, 64, 65
  symbolism of, 15
  in When Stars Collide, 60, 61, 158, 159
Yellow-green, 136, 138, 140
  in Autumn Glow, 112, 113, 216, 217
  in Romantica, 64, 65
  in SpinWheels, 76, 77, 151, 152, 153
  in Two Colors Separated by Four Colors harmony, 95
Yellow-orange, 138
  in Amethyst and Jade, 42, 43, 237, 238
  in Autumn Glow, 112, 113, 216, 217
  in Butterflies Are Free, 52, 53, 144, 145
  in Mardi Gras, 108, 109
  in Mystic Garden, 48, 49
  in Rosewood, 80, 81
  in SpinWheels, 76, 77, 151, 152, 153
  in Star Bright, 88, 89
  in Star Dance, 68, 69, 228, 229
  in When Stars Collide, 60, 61, 158, 159